A Century of New England in

# News Photos

A Century of New England in

# News Photos

By John Harris

The
Globe
Pequot
Press

Old Chester Road
Chester, Connecticut 06412

Old *Globe* — Original building
where Gen. Chas. H. Taylor
developed the *Globe,* 1872-1887,
until it was replaced by a 7-story
structure, then the tallest in old
Newspaper Row.

## *ABBREVIATIONS*

AP – Associated Press
BPL – Boston Public Library
CHS – Connecticut Historical Society
LC – Library of Congress
NHHS – N.H. Historical Society
RIHS – R.I. Historical Society
UPI – United Press International

## *THE BOSTON GLOBE*

Copyright © The Globe Newspaper Co.
First Edition      All Rights Reserved
Published in Chester, CT by the Globe Pequot Press
ISBN: 0-87106-024-8
Library of Congress Catalog Number: 79-50261
Manufactured in the United States of America

Designed by Peter and Janet Good

A Century of New England in

# News Photos

Contents:

## INTRODUCTION

Like music and dancing, newsmen and news photographers go together as naturally as newspapers and Newspaper Row to provide their exciting product:

News photographs and headlines.

As long as this writer had been in newspaper work – and this goes back to the late 1920's – the adventure of a news story usually started with a news flash in the City Room. In those days reporter and photographer most often raced off together, and this newsman at times held the flash powder tray aloft while the cameraman literally "banged" his news shot.

Times change. In the current age of specialization, newsmen and photographers often work independently. Still the link between Dark Room and City Room is everlastingly present. Photos have to be processed to catch edition times and editors have to decide which are to be the ones that go to press.

Newsman, news editor, news executive – your writer has filled all these roles for half a century on the staff of New England's largest newspaper, the *Boston Globe.* This book is the most recent in a series of books that I have successively prepared for our readers by locating photographs and writing text.

This time, at first, I thought securing the pictures would be a comparatively easy task. The *Boston Globe*'s library has the largest collection of news clips and news photos in this part of the nation. This library, from my experience with libraries, is beyond any doubt the most resourceful news library in New England, and every uncredited photograph in this book came from it.

But from the number of other credits appended to the captions you will readily observe that photographs of many news events could be presented only through the kindness of many other sources. This is because every photo in this book had to be reproduced from an original – a taxing demand for even the finest of news libraries.

The search for those originals has led me through stacks of photo files dating back to the infancy of photojournalism.

And so, on the first page of each of the four sections comprising this book I have briefly recounted the development of photography and of reproduction of photographs in the daily newspaper. In this age of instant everything it may be surprising to recall that many of the discoveries that made picture making possible have come in comparatively recent times.

In the era of the first *Boston Globe,* in the early 1870's, we were still in the days of glass plate photography, and no process was then known on how to reproduce in news columns anything other than woodcuts.

Photographs, of course, best illustrate the unsuspected problems of early photojournalism. A whirling waterspout, a sensational sight, appears on page 31. Indeed, that 1896 marvel is believed to have been the most-photographed waterspout in history, for among the thousands of vacationers who saw it were scores of photography fans.

Now that we have grown accustomed to instantaneous photos (even instant movies and replays), the amazing advances in photography are certainly underscored by the fact that that waterspout appeared and disappeared three distinct times within the space of 30 minutes. Yet cameras of that era were so cumbersome to set up and focus that, though the first appearance lasted 13 minutes, there was not a single photograph made. But the camera fans were ready and succeeded on the waterspout's genie-like reappearances.

Photojournalism was quick to develop, and steel-nerved stunts of news cameramen have since provided legends in newspaper offices across the land. The exploit of *Globe* cameraman Eddie Bond (the tale is in the text) snapping a Boston panorama while dangling from a plank held by a friend atop the 220-foot-high Bunker Hill Monument has always thrilled me. My search for that original photograph was intensive but in vain.

Just in recent years we have a similar stunt roughly four times higher above terra firma.

For the photograph, glance at page 126. The view is of the topping-off of New England's currently highest structure, the John Hancock Insurance Company building in Boston. To get some perspective on the 790 feet of air between the construction worker and the hard ground, notice in the background the entire lower basin of the quite broad Charles River.

The height was so perilous that construction insurance did not cover the *Globe* cameraman above the next lower level. So the insurance company press agent, while refusing permission for any visiting newsmen to go to the top level, obligingly took the focused camera and made the shot – a shot that later caused the construction worker's wife to faint rather promptly.

Few things on earth can stir emotions and memories with the effectiveness of photographs, and in browsing through this book you just may do as much reminiscing as reading.

My years as the *Globe*'s political editor and Washington correspondent have brought close acquaintance with, and vivid recollection of, many public figures.

FDR, Franklin Delano Roosevelt, bestrode his era in a way colossal and magnetic. The happy confidence on his smiling face when he would proclaim a "New Deal" for a depression-weary nation (p. 71) and the candor of his fireside chats (p. 74) made his leadership seem omnipotent. The wearing cares of office showed on his face clearly in later years (p. 88), and near the end I would notice his arm, laboriously raised to light a cigarette, fall like a lifeless weight.

I remember watching embattled President Harry S. Truman (p. 98) speaking to a stupendous crowd from the front steps of Providence, Rhode Island's city hall. People were listening from every window and packed tight on the ground for as far as the eye could see. It was in the final days of the 1948 Presidential race in which the polls proclaimed Truman would lose to Thomas E. Dewey of New York, and Dewey was due to speak the next day in Providence.

"There's a man following me around," Truman remarked, and then raising his voice in his best never-say-die manner he added, "And I want to tell you that that's where he'll be on election day...Following me!" The throng, in delight, roared enthusiastic approval – and must have gone to the polls and voted to keep Harry in the White House.

For skill in speaking it would be difficult to top Winston Churchill. See him waving from Harvard's chapel steps (p. 85). During his brief visit that day he lived up to his hearty tankard reputation by downing several glasses of brandy at lunch and shortly thereafter walked across the Harvard yard to big Memorial Hall for a radio address to literally the entire world.

The time: right on the eve of the momentous 1943 Allied invasion of Italy. In front of him, as it looked in those days, was a forest of competing microphones to catch his voice.

Churchill spoke flawlessly, composing his words as he went, and I saw that he never even glanced at the little white prompt card in his hand. A giant among orators, he was literally the master consummate of the English tongue.

For emotion and nostalgia, few photographs are as poignant as the scene (p.108) after the wedding of Jacqueline and John F. Kennedy. The wedding banquet on the spacious lawn overlooking the sparkling bay seemed to me like festivity in Camelot, with all its music and youth, laughter and toasts in champagne. Then all too soon the bereavement (pp.115,124) when the two brothers, groom and best man that glamorous day, were brought down by assassins.

You will find that episodes in the growth of the *Boston Globe* are associated with this presentation of photographs and news photography, so a bit more about the *Globe*.

It was not always the largest newspaper in New England. It had to win that responsibility over the years.

A century-plus after the founding of the *Globe* it is still a family newspaper. In that span the post of publisher has passed in the Taylor family three times from father to son. This is mighty exceptional and remarkable in American journalism.

The first Taylor, Gen. Charles H. Taylor, was a young Civil War veteran when he started the *Globe* on old Newspaper Row, near what was once the center of old colonial government. The whole area teemed with rival newspapers then, and the general's sincere regard for people, for the community and civic life, steadily won friends for the *Globe*. He sought to keep abreast of every improvement possible for his paper, but it was a full five years of strug-gle before it was free from debt and on its way.

The general's oldest son and namesake developed what was among the nation's first, or possibly the very first, photo-engraving facility to make possible the printing of illustrations in news columns.

In 1875 the *Globe* ran its first cartoon.

Soon to follow were news illustrations, and last but not least, news photos. They changed the face of the *Globe* and of every newspaper in New England.

Turn a few pages, and you'll see how.

JOHN HARRIS

## ABOUT THE AUTHOR

JOHN HARRIS, born in Boston in 1908, is a graduate of the nation's two oldest schools, Boston Public Latin School and Harvard University. Save for service in the Navy in World War II he has been a lifetime member of the staff of the *Boston Globe*, where he has been political editor, Washington correspondent, Sunday editor and associate editor.

American history has been his special interest, and he has written extensively about it in articles, booklets and books, including "Walks in Washington," "Presidential Libraries," "Massachusetts Constitutional Convention," the history portions of *Treasures of Massachusetts* and "The Great Boston Fire—1872," as well as a series of books on the American Revolution.

He is currently writing a book on early American colonial settlements.

# News Photos

# 1872–1900

## Illustrating in an Age of Marvels

In November of 1872 – the year in which the *Boston Globe* commenced publication – Boston's commercial center was literally consumed by the most devastating fire in the annals of New England.

The flames swept beyond control for 20 hours through block after block of wholesale and retail business structures, leaving ruins, injured and dead. They ravaged more than 65 acres in the heart of the city extending from its main thoroughfare, Washington Street, to its harbor.

The cost of the blaze per acre, even compared to the more extensive Chicago conflagration of just a year earlier, set a record that was said in that period to have made Boston's loss "unparalleled by any fire of ancient or modern times." Fire apparatus sped by road or by railway flatcar from all over New England, save from far-off Vermont. Photographers, too, flocked to Boston – not only from New England, but from all over the nation.

Countless pictures, professional and amateur, were made. They exist still in great numbers. Yet not one of these depictions of the great holocaust portrays any action. Film fast enough to preserve the furious progress of the flames, the panic of the people, the desperate struggle of the firefighters, did not exist. Any motion simply blurred old glass-type plates.

Moreover, no process had been perfected at that time to reproduce photographs in newspapers. (The *Globe,* unlike some less fortunate Boston newspapers, escaped with its plant intact.) Fast film that would initiate the era of snapshots as well as a photo-engraving technique to print the photographer's work in the daily newspaper were then both years away.

The *Boston Globe* got started in the seemingly more leisurely days of hand-set type, gas lights and horse-drawn streetcars. Still, the camera, a product of the 19th century, had made comparatively rapid strides since the 1830s when Louis Daguerre, a Frenchman, revealed a way to preserve images. By mid-century a British sculptor, Frederick Archer, invented a process, the "wet plate," that displaced the daguerreo-type picture. This process, universally, was the basis of picture taking when the *Globe* was born and continued well into the 1880s.

All early photographic methods were costly and cumbersome. Daguerre's exposures took fully 20 minutes – quite an ordeal to sit still for a portrait. Clamps, of course, helped. In the years that followed, the havoc, carnage and battlefield sights of the Crimean War were preserved in pictures. Widely known are the scenes of our Civil War photographed by Matthew Brady and his associates. Still no movement could be preserved.

The revolutionary discovery in 1871 of the "dry plate" process – with exposures possible in a fraction of a second – would lead in the 1890s to George Eastman's photographic film, his Kodak camera and snapshots.

How did the newspapers illustrate news events in the early days? Only one way existed: Sketches and illustrations. They were made at first on woodblocks and later on metal. Usage of them had a very slow growth. The *Globe* became a pioneer in photo-engraving and one of the first newspaper plants with picture-making facilities. But it was not until the year of the nation's centennial, 1875, that the *Globe* was able to achieve illustrations in its news columns and ran its first cartoon.

Lizzie Borden's sensational, summertime trial for murder in 1893 is a classic example of the state of newspaper illustration. The *Globe* already had a busy staff of photographers. The public was eager to be shown every detail of the trial. Photographs were rushed from New Bedford, site of the trial, to Boston. Still only sketches appeared. "Caught by a *Globe* camera" is the headline over one. It meant: Copied from a photograph.

The zinc plate process for printing halftones in news columns was still in the future.

When looking back from modern times to the final decades of the last century there is a tendency to regard them blandly as comparatively a period of tranquility, easy-going, little-doing. This was emphatically not the way they were described by the *Globe* when it celebrated its first quarter-century with a special supplement in 1897. They were portrayed, indeed, as: "An age of marvels!"

Thomas Edison, then in his inventive heyday, announced in what seemed rapid succession his devising a phonograph, electric light bulb and motion pictures. Alexander Graham Bell invented his telephone – in downtown Boston. Boston produced the country's first American-made bicycles. An awed nation was first given telegraphy without wires, electric street cars, electric elevators. Typewriters came to city rooms and in medicine there came the wonder of the X ray.

There were milestones as well as wonders – national milestones that thrilled New Englanders. Brooklyn Bridge was opened. The cornerstone of the Statue of Liberty was set in place on Bedloe's Island and the capstone was mounted on the Washington Monument.

Color embellished this special supplement in 1897. Three years earlier the *Globe* had commenced using the first color press installed in New England, printing at a speed of 12,000 copies an hour, a speed that seemed magical for its day. It made possible color in comics. Sophisticated reproduction of color photographs in newspapers, however, would not be possible until the far-off 1930s.

A curious fact about the advent of halftones (full newspaper photographic reproduction) was that opposition arose within the newspaper fraternity to their use.

Some staid newspapers rejected them even into the Twentieth Century. They felt there was something upstart about them! Nowadays we have come to treasure old photographs, even when the names of the people have been lost, for photographs – and sketches based on them – offer the most vivid and authentic way to recapture the appearance and events of earlier America.

*CONFLAGRATION SCENES*
*in Boston Nov. 9-11, 1872*

*a*    Terror-stricken, a young woman clerk leaps to her death.

*b*    East Boston's 1872 Engine 11 called the *John S. Damrell* for Boston's fire chief who directed the fight against the flames. (Bostonian Society)

*c*    Merchants in Chauncey Street, near start of the fire, protect their wares against looters.

*d*    Water streams forced by Kearsarge 3 pumper immediately after its arrival from Manchester, N.H. save Old South Meeting House from the 1872 conflagration. (Boston Athenaeum)

*a*

*b*

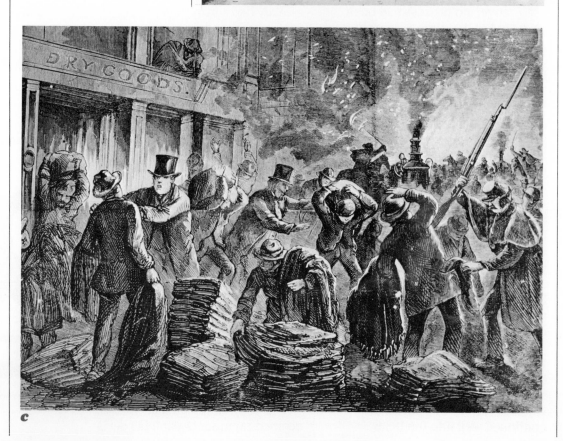

*c*

d

*a*　The *Globe*'s first portrait illustration, May 29, 1875, shows trial view of Jesse H. Pomeroy, 16-year-old notorious child-killer and torturer, who spent 56 of his 72 years in prison, 41 of them in solitary confinement. He died in 1932 after serving longer than any other American lifer.

*b*　Ashes and ruins – a loss, in modern terms, of more than $500 million – as seen from the waterfront in foreground, stretching back to Washington Street, from Summer Street on the left to State Street on the right, an area that hours earlier contained the commercial heart of the metropolis and of New England. (Boit, Dalton & Church Inc.)

*c*　"Daylight through the mountain" – At 3:20 p.m. on Nov. 27, 1873 a final blast of 150 pounds of nitroglycerine cleared the last rock to complete a 5-mile tunnel through Hoosac Mountain, in the Berkshires, and open a new route between "the great West and…New England." A labor of 17 years, it is one of America's longest tunnels. (AP)

out of the way of even repeating his crimes, there are many other people who argue that it would be a blot on the good name and fair fame of the old Bay State to have it recorded that her men, in high places, have hung a boy! Many people in South Boston and Chelsea are familiar with the personal appearance of the youth, but many of our thousands of readers are not; hence we present a likeness of him, this morning, which will, undoubtedly, be readily recognized as truthful by those familiar with his look.

**Pomeroy's Career of Crime.**

The story of the bloody deeds and inhuman butcheries of this boy, who has earned the title of " the boy fiend," will not soon be effaced from the memories of the people of this generation, at least, and his name will be used in the household, as it has been, as a terror to refractory children. Notwithstanding the fact that the story has been so often told, it is not inopportune at the present time, in view of the facts above stated to briefly recount the terrible crimes that have rendered Pomeroy famous in criminal history. If the thirst for human blood and delight in witnessing the sufferings of others

*a*

*b*

## OUR NATION'S FIRST CENTENNIAL, APRIL 19, 1875

"Welcome to the Birthplace of American Liberty" graced an arch on the Battle Green at Lexington. Two big tents were erected, one for a banquet of 3500 guests headed by President Ulysses S. Grant, the other seating 7000. Despite the freezing, bitter weather some 100,000 spectators jammed into the small community.

**a** The *Globe* on June 17, 1875, the 100th anniversary of the Battle of Bunker Hill, published its first cartoon, a post-Civil War appeal for North and South to live in peace.

**b** New marble statues of patriots Samuel Adams and John Hancock were unveiled and appeared in the *Globe* as its first news illustrations.

**c** The centennial setting on Lexington's Battle Green. (Cary Memorial Library, Lexington)

**d** Concord drew similar "immense crowds" and also entertained the President. Poet Ralph Waldo Emerson told of fellow townsman Daniel Chester French, 25, creating his "Minuteman" statue then being unveiled near the bridge. (Concord Free Library)

THE NORTH TO THE SOUTH, GREETING:
BRETHREN, LET US DWELL TOGETHER IN UNITY.

*a*

The Decorations.

The entrance to the tent is under an arch which bears the inscription: "Welcome to the Birthplace of American Liberty!" and the figures 1775 and 1875. From the liberty pole on the green, lines of flags and bunting are hung over Bedford and Monument streets. On one flag is inscribed:
"Don't fire unless fired upon, but if they mean to have war, let it begin here."—*Captain Parker.*

*b*

*c*

*d*

a

## EMINENT IN NEW ENGLAND

*a*   "Mark Twain," pen name for Samuel L. Clemens (1835-1910), created classic American boys Tom Sawyer and Huckleberry Finn. With little formal education, Twain tried being everything, a printer's devil, Mississippi pilot, gold-miner and journalist. Here he is pictured with his family on the porch of his Hartford, Conn., riverboat-style mansion, now a museum. (Mark Twain Memorial, Hartford)

*b*   Henry Wadsworth Longfellow (1807-1882)—"Listen, my children and you shall hear"— was a poet and professor at Bowdoin College and Harvard. Among his best-loved creations are "Hiawatha," *Evangeline* and *Tales of a Wayside Inn.* He is shown with a daughter on the front steps of his home in Cambridge, Revolutionary headquarters of George Washington and now a museum. (Longfellow National Historical Site)

*c*   Clara Barton (1821-1912) founded the American Red Cross in 1881. She quit her government job, served as a nurse on Civil War battlefields and later pioneered Red Cross help in times of civilian disasters. Here Miss Barton is photographed on a visit to her birthplace at Oxford, Mass.

b

c

*d*    Julia Ward Howe (1819-1910) here is seated in her Beacon Street home, an intellectual center of 19th century Boston. Philanthropist, editor, suffragette, she is best remembered for her poem "Battle Hymn of the Republic."

*e*    Phineas Taylor Barnum (1810-1891), skillful in his youth as a practical joker, became in his 30's America's greatest showman. From funds accumulated by stage-managing a midget called Tom Thumb and presenting Jenny Lind, the "Swedish Nightingale," P.T. created a three-ring circus he dubbed "The Greatest Show on Earth" – and retired to a great villa in Bridgeport, Conn.

*f*    Ralph Waldo Emerson (1803-1882), clergyman and descendant of a long line of clergymen, was a leader in the famous Concord Group of authors including Louisa May Alcott, Nathaniel Hawthorne and Henry David Thoreau.

*g*    Frederick Douglass (1817-1875) escaped from Southern slavery, worked as a day laborer in New Bedford, appeared at the Massachusetts Anti-Slavery Society Convention at Nantucket and joined its advocates in Boston. Self-taught, he became a journalist, lecturer, publisher and fighter for women's suffrage. (Museum of Afro-American History, Boston)

*h*    Winslow Homer (1836-1910), a battle-front sketch artist in the Civil War, attained his greatest fame as a marine painter of the coast of Maine and the Caribbean. Homer, shown in his studio at Prout's Neck, Me., is about to complete a famous canvas, "Gulf Stream." (Bowdoin College)

*i*    John Singer Sargent (1856-1925), painter, was educated abroad and spent most of his life there, but his greatest murals are to be seen in centers of New England culture such as Boston's Public Library and the Museum of Fine Arts. (National Academy of Design)

*d*

*e*

*f*

*g*

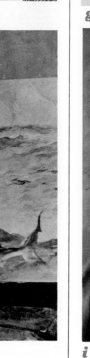

*h*

*i*

*a*    President Grover Cleveland's favorite relaxation: fishing off Gray Gables, his vacation home on Cape Cod. (Mrs. Esther Cleveland Bosanquet)

*b*    Vermont-born Chester A. Arthur became President Sept. 20, 1881, when President James A. Garfield was assassinated. (AP)

*c*    Telephone's birthplace – Prof. Bell's 5th floor attic workbench at 109 Court St. where on June 3, 1875 he first sent a human voice over a telephone wire.

*d*    John L. Sullivan, ex-plumber's helper, became American heavyweight champ on Feb. 7, 1882 by knocking out Paddy Ryan in the 9th round of a bare knuckles bout in Mississippi. (LC)

*e*    Sullivan, "the Boston Strong Boy," in later life preached against "Demon Rum" and raised flowers in his retirement at West Abington, Mass.

a

b

c

e

d

**a** Columbia, a high-wheeler introduced in England in 1871 eight years before the modern chain bike, was first sold in America by Boston shoe manufacturer Albert A. Pope, who opened the first American bicycle factory. (Transportation Museum)

**b** America's first automobile — Bicycle-maker Charles E. Duryea, 32, operates his new invention — a two-horsepower gasoline engine attached to a ladies' phaeton — which he first demonstrated on the streets of Springfield, Mass., Sept. 21, 1893 with people flocking to see a carriage move "with no shafts and no horse." (LC)

**c** Boston got the first electric street cars in New England in 1888, three years after the pioneer ones ran in Baltimore, Md. (Mrs. Bessie M. Hunt)

**d** Bennington, Vt., was bedecked with flags Aug. 19, 1891 as President Harrison and New England governors dedicated the new, towering 308-foot Bennington Battle Monument to mark the victory of Gen. John Stark that made possible the crucial, turning-point victory of the American Revolution at Saratoga. Monument as it neared completion. (Tyler Resch)

**d**

*a*

*b*

*THE YEAR 1888
BROUGHT STORMS SO
SEVERE THAT THE TERM
"BLIZZARD" CAME INTO
WIDESPREAD USE.*

Fierce winds with sudden drops in temperature to low sub-zero froze farmers in fields, children enroute to school and wayfarers in snowdrifts. One blizzard struck, dropping up to 50 inches of snow, spreading chaos and death from March 11-14, choking highways, stalling and burying trains, severing communication.

*a* Wind-swept snow, like a mountain peak, in front of old Federal building (now lawn of old State House) looking uphill on State Street, Hartford, Conn. (CHS)

*b* Cartoons and sketches brought *Globe* readers the local story.

*c* "The Great Drift," 15 feet high, on Hartford's Clinton Street with 6'3" tunnel and 10-foot arch.

This photograph, made two days after the blizzard, was sent to newspapers around the nation as proof of the extraordinary aftermath of this New England storm. Clinton Street, in the heart of downtown Hartford, is a block east on Capitol Avenue from the Connecticut State Capitol.

Between 20 and 50 inches of snow fell in Connecticut Mar. 11 and 12, then more snow came the next day, accompanied by furious, gale-force northwest winds that piled "drifts 20 to 40 feet by actual measurement." Workers were trapped in office buildings and people in their houses. Trains with their mushroom-like smoke stacks were stranded for days. There was no mail, no burials, no horse-drawn streetcars. Milkmen fought drifts to try to bring milk to babies.

The telephone and a drop in crime were about the only comforts, and a week passed before emergency snow shovelers could clear narrow channels through all the main streets. (CHS, *Hartford Courant*)

*c*

a

*a* Eighty acres in Lynn's central business section – then the nation's top shoe manufacturing center – were gutted by fire that started at noon Nov. 26, 1889 in the engine room of a 5-story wooden shoe factory. Winds of "terrible" intensity spread the flames. Soon blocks of the city's finest buildings and the main depot were debris and ashes. Hundreds of residents were made homeless. (Lynn Historical Soc.)

*b* A cyclone struck the southside tenement district of Lawrence, Mass., at 9:15 a.m. July 26, 1890 and within three minutes cut a swath 300 feet wide, nearly a mile long and left in it eight dead, 28 wounded crying for help, 100 wrecked houses. The only warning was a few black clouds in a downpour. (Merrimack Valley Textile Museum)

*c* Death from scalding steam was the fate of 29 passengers, while 47 others were injured in the 9-car train when the Old Colony's express from Wood's Hole jumped the track near Dimmock Street bridge, Quincy, Aug. 19, 1890. A track jack, left by workmen scurrying from the express' path, caused the derailment. (Quincy Public Library)

*b*

*c*

*a*

*A CLASSIC MURDER TRIAL BEGAN JUNE 5, 1893 IN NEW BEDFORD WHEN LIZZIE BORDEN, 32-YEAR-OLD HEIRESS, STOOD BEFORE HER JUDGES AND JURY.*

A popular jingle epitomizes the accusations against her:
　"Lizzie Borden took an axe
　And gave her mother forty whacks.
　When she saw what she had done
　She gave her father forty-one."
　Interest in her fate was widespread. The *Globe*, with no method available for printing photographs (though its photographers made many), used sketches made from photos. The sensational court proceedings dominated the headlines until the trial ended in her acquittal June 21.

*a*　Photo of Lizzie. (Fall River Public Library)

*b*　Lizzie's jail cell.

*c*　Lizzie leaving the courthouse during trial.

*d*　Lizzie listening to the verdict.

*b*

c

d

*a*

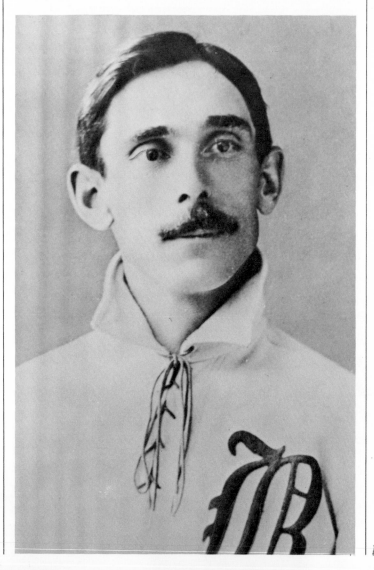

*b*

*a*   Walter Camp, "Father of Football," starred as halfback at Yale, later coached there, created rules for intercollegiate football. (Yale)

*b*   In the second game of a double-header on May 20, 1894 Robert "Link" Lowe, 25, and in his fifth season with the Boston Nationals (later the Boston Braves) became the first man to belt four home runs in a single game. Two came in the third inning.

*COLOR FOR LIVELINESS WAS OFFERED TO ITS READERS WHEN THE GLOBE INSTALLED THE FIRST NEWS- PAPER COLOR PRESS IN NEW ENGLAND IN 1894 AND DIS- TRIBUTED ITS FIRST COLOR SUPPLEMENT ON NOV. 25.*

**c**  During the "Gay Nineties" the Harvard-Yale annual football clash was just about at the peak of social events. That Nov. 25, the day of the game, the *Globe* presented the players of both teams in color, not knowing of course how the game would come out. Harvard took a shel- lacking 12-4 in a game so rough that some players were injured.

**d**  On Sundays that followed Nov. 25, the *Globe* ran two full pages in color illustrations based on photos that present a most vivid record of how some activities and people appeared in the 1890s. Here, firemen speed through Boston's old Scollay Square to an 1894 fire.

*c*

*d*

*a*

*b*

***a***   The *Portland,* built at Bath, Maine, in 1890 (Peabody Museum, Salem).

***b***   "THE NIGHT THE *PORTLAND* WENT DOWN" – Ignoring warnings, the skipper of the *Portland*, 280-foot, side-paddle steamer, left Boston's India Wharf at 7 p.m. Nov. 26, 1898 for his regular nightly Boston-Portland run. Every one of the 163 on board, captain, crew and passengers, would perish.
The *Portland* had barely disappeared into the darkness when a northeaster struck. Winds reached frightful 70-mph force, snow poured down, waves became mountainous, producing marine disasters up and down the New England coast. Fate of the *Portland* did not become clear until nearly three days after the storm's onslaught when bodies, life preservers, freight and wreckage were washed ashore on outer Cape Cod. The *Portland*, last spotted by a fisherman off Rockport, had apparently become disabled and been swept helplessly southward, going down off the Cape's Highland Light.

***c***   Sea spectacular – A waterspout, a whirling column stretching from the surface of the ocean to the clouds, as it appeared off Oak Bluffs, Martha's Vineyard, on Aug. 19, 1896. (LC)
Most remarkably, this waterspout, 3600 feet high and 140 feet at its center, moved six miles offshore and was seen by the largest audience ever to view such a phenomenon – thousands of mid-summer visitors all along the western shore of Martha's Vineyard. Such spouts are more awesome than destructive usually, but the sight left many women and children in hysterics. (LC)

***d***   Old Fall River line – In 1894 the popular overnight sea run from Fall River to New York City, then nearly a half century old, added its most palatial vessel, *S.S. Priscilla*, described as "not so large as an ocean liner but quite as sumptuous." (Marine Museum at Fall River).

***c***

***d***

# THE GLOBE EXTRA!

## LATEST

# FIRST CAR OFF THE EARTH.

## Allston Electric Goes Into the Subway on Schedule Time.

THE CROWDED FIRST CAR AT THE SUBWAY ENTRANCE.

*a*

*AMERICA'S FIRST STREET-CAR SUBWAY WAS OPENED SEPT. 1, 1897, PUTTING AN END TO THE MILE-AN-HOUR TRAFFIC CONGESTION THAT HAD VIRTUALLY BLOCKADED BOSTON'S BUSY DOWNTOWN TREMONT STREET.*

Only a third of the planned 1.7 miles of underground was finished—from the Public Garden to Park Street—and had taken two-and-a-half years.

***a*** One hundred cheering passengers were crowded into the first car to enter the subway, a car from Allston via Cambridge, Harvard Bridge and Boylston Street, due daily at Park Street at 6:01 a.m.

***b*** "Hail to the hero!"— Admiral George Dewey, Spanish-American War idol for sinking the Spanish Fleet in Manila Bay, was given an unprecedented welcome in Boston Oct. 13-14, 1899. Dewey, a native of Montpelier, Vt., dedicated a cornerstone at Vermont's Norwich University, where he got his early training, before arriving at Boston. Governors of the New England states greeted him along his triumphant New England route and accompanied him at parades, receptions and banquets. Dewey, in full dress uniform, doffs his hat to the throng along Boston's Charles Street.

***c*** "Gold in the Klondike!"— Word of gold discovered late in 1896 in Rabbit Creek—quickly renamed Bonanza Creek—drew a stampede the next year to Alaska. Hundreds of houses sprang up in Dawson City where in 1896 there had been but a single hut. It was like a re-run of the '49-er rush to California, drawing fortune-seekers, too, from all over New England. Scene: Haverhill, Mass., group en route to Dawson City.

*b*

*c*

a

b

*a*    Secretary of State James G. Blaine, "The Shining Knight of Maine," in 1889 welcomes to his summer home at Bar Harbor, Maine, his chief, the newly elected President Benjamin Harrison and the elder Senator Henry Cabot Lodge with members of their families. *Back Row:* (l to r) Lodge, Walker Blaine, presidential secretary E.W. Halford. *Front Row:* James Blaine Jr., Mrs. Lodge, the President, Mrs. Blaine, Miss Harriett Blaine. (Maine Historical Society)

*b*    Boston's last horsecar, on its final run Dec. 24, 1900 to the Public Garden, paused on Dartmouth street beside the descendant church of the Old South Meeting House in Boston's Copley Square. (Robert Stanley)

*c*    Two Bishops — Rev. Phillips Brooks, Episcopal bishop of Massachusetts (right) and his successor, Rev. William Lawrence, as they crossed Boston Common in 1892 in a snapshot made by the *Globe*'s first photographer, John W. Butters, the first regular newspaper photographer in New England.

c

# News Photos

# 1901–1932

## Into the New Century

Now, in the early years of the 1900s, came swift changes.

The horsecar gave way increasingly to the electric streetcar in community after community.

Automobiles, their early wonders becoming commonplace with wider usage, were soon eclipsed in public attention by the Wright Brothers' conquest of the air. To advance aviation, the *Boston Globe* offered prizes as it had done in its earliest days for bicycle and automobile competitions.

And the perfecting of engraving techniques made it at last possible for the public to expect news photographs to illustrate its daily newspaper.

Cameramen, with the immeasurably easier rolls of speedy film that Eastman made possible, could go in for stunts. Some are well remembered. Globeman Edmunds "Eddie" Bond rigged a miniature camera of his own an astounding two decades before the Leica miniature camera made its appearance in 1925. Bond, concealing this novelty behind his vest, snapped courtroom scenes of notorious murderers Charles Tucker and Harry K. Thaw.

Bond's most sensational camera stunt was performed in 1907 at the top of 220-foot Bunker Hill Monument. An editor showed Bond a panoramic view of Boston sketched by an artist from atop the monument in 1848. Bond offered to show the intervening changes from the same elevation, an unprecedented offer.

At the time there were repairs being made and the iron bars had been removed from the small, narrow windows in the monument's summit room at the head of the 295 winding stone steps. Bond slid a plank out the south window, braced it with a second plank, had a friend steady it, then went out on the plank.

Holding camera in both hands, standing with more than 200 feet of air between him and the ground, Bond coolly snapped the view, from the old Charlestown Navy Yard on his left to the gold-topped State House on his right—and had the first successful photograph from the monument's top.

Yarns like this retold in the newspaper's city room spurred reporters to match stunts with scoops. One scoop will suffice:

New England, with many families agonized by lack of solid news, was among the areas especially distraught by word of the sinking of the White Star liner *Titanic* with a loss of some 1500 lives. Reports of the number of survivors picked up by the Cunard liner *Carpathia* varied from 655 to 868.

What was the true figure? The *Globe* found that another Cunard liner, the *Franconia,* was just about to sail from Boston to Europe. The yachting editor, who knew sea captains, was quickly sent aboard, for the *Franconia* within 24 hours should be within wireless contact both of the *Carpathia* and of Boston. At that point at sea the yachting editor was able to transmit a world scoop that named a total of exactly 705. (He then went on to England and happy sessions with his old friend and fellow yachtsman Sir Thomas Lipton.)

Inventions steadily provided milestones. When the first, pioneer airmail plane left Washington for Boston on Aug. 9, 1923 the *Globe* cameramen managed to send back photos of scenes as Coolidge took over the White House after the death of Harding. On March 4, 1929 when bleak weather iced and grounded planes, the *Globe* camera-

men were able to dispatch to Boston pictures of Herbert Hoover's inaugural by telephoto—and fancy a day this could be done by radio.

In city rooms the most vivid memory about cameramen in this period is of their using magnesium flashpowder, inflammable powder poured on a tray, held overhead and ignited, boom! The procedure was extremely dangerous and provided but little control over the quality of light. But it and its horror tales, became passe when the amazing flash bulb, built of aluminum foil, was invented in 1929.

*Left*: Every New England state was represented and one million people cheered when the war-scarred, khaki-clad veterans of the 26th Yankee Division, 21,000 strong, marched for more than four hours through Boston streets April 25, 1919 on their return home from World War I. Wounded veterans led the parade.

*a*     A new, more powerful era for the U.S. Presidency began Sept. 14, 1901 in the library of a Buffalo mansion when Theodore "Teddy" Roosevelt, 42, heroic colonel of the "Rough Riders," was sworn in as Chief Executive upon the death of President William McKinley, shot eight days earlier by an assassin. Scene sketched by *Globe* artist.

*b*     President Roosevelt escaped sudden death Sept. 3, 1902 a half-mile outside Pittsfield, Mass., when his open landau drawn by four white horses was struck by an electric streetcar "speeding at 30 mph." TR, jolted from the carriage, was bruised, cut and shaken. His driver was gravely injured. A secret serviceman, flung under streetcar's wheels, was instantly killed. (Berkshire Athenaeum)

*c*     The President's 1902 tour of New England was part of his effort to let the nation become acquainted with its new President. TR, escorted by local police on bicycles, greets throngs of well-wishers along Pearl Street, a main avenue in Hartford, Conn.
He spoke at the Hartford Coliseum Aug. 22 and arrived on the presidential yacht from Oyster Bay to begin his New England tour in New Haven earlier that day. By Sept. 3, when he reboarded his yacht *Sylph*, he had spoken in nearly every large community in all six states, making as many as half a dozen speeches a day.
All this time, inexhaustible TR was also busy settling a crippling national coal strike, which he accomplished Oct. 3 while confined at last to a wheelchair as a result of his ignoring injuries sustained in Pittsfield on the final day of his tour. (CHS)

*c*

*a*    Flames destroyed a large part of the business center of Waterbury, Conn., Feb. 2-3, 1902. Carried by strong winds, the fire burned block after block of stores and tenements leaving hundreds homeless, millions in damage. (Mattatach Hist. Soc.)

*b*    Like an atomic blast, two powder magazines of the U.S. Cartridge shops of Tewksbury (then part of So. Lowell) exploded shortly after 9 a.m., July 29, 1903, blowing 19 persons to bits, horribly injuring 50 more and flattening some 15 homes. Cause unknown. (Lowell Museum)

*c*    In the worst Bay State fire since Boston's center was destroyed in 1872, fully one-fourth of Chelsea was devastated April 12, 1908 when flames swept over 275 acres for 10 hours. Nineteen residents lost their lives, hundreds were injured. Chelsea's city hall, library and new hospital were left in ashes, 2822 buildings destroyed, 15,000 homeless. Scene: Householders flee before the flames.

*a*

*b*

c

*FIRST WIRELESS MESSAGE FROM THE U.S. TO EUROPE WAS SENT JAN. 18, 1903 BY THE INVENTOR GUGLIELMO MARCONI FROM SOUTH WELLFLEET ON CAPE COD TO ENGLAND, A GREETING FROM PRESIDENT TEDDY ROOSEVELT TO KING EDWARD VI.*

*a*    First South Wellfleet station.

*b*    Guglielmo Marconi *(left)*.

*c*    Old Newspaper Row, on lower Washington Street, was always a magnet for news-hungry Greater Bostonians. Here on Nov. 5, 1907 a throng devours the latest returns (former *Globe* buildings on the left) as Republican Gov. Curtis Guild Jr. triumphs over divided Democrats to win a third term.

*a*

b

c

*a*

*b*

*a*    Lord Dartmouth, a great-great-grandson of the Earl of Dartmouth for whom Dartmouth College was named, came to Hanover, N.H., Oct. 26, 1904, to lay the cornerstone of new Dartmouth Hall. The visitor, sixth earl, (*left*) made a gift of family correspondence relating to the college's creation. (Dartmouth)

*b*    Treaty of Portsmouth—Through President Roosevelt's initiative, a peace treaty was signed Sept. 5, 1905 at the Portsmouth, N.H. Navy Yard, ending the 1904-1905 Russo-Japanese War. TR, who later was awarded the Nobel Peace prize, poses with Russian and Japanese diplomats. (Sagamore Hill Nat'l Hist. Site)

*c*    Hartford's Bulkeley Bridge, named for Conn. Gov. Morgan Gardner Bulkeley, was the longest true stone arch bridge in the nation when completed in 1908 to replace a fire-ravaged covered wooden bridge that spanned the Connecticut River. Dedication included a 17th century settlers' pageant. (CHS)

*d*    Cape Cod Canal, a dream of the earliest 17th century settlers, was begun in 1909 and opened to traffic July 29, 1914. The excursion boat "Rose Standish," loaded with dignitaries, steams on opening day through the new canal, followed by a torpedo boat destroyer and eight yachts.

c

d

*a*  Three years after man learned to fly at Kitty Hawk, the balloon ascent — popular since France's King Louis XVI in 1783 watched the first one — continued to draw delighted crowds. Scene: Old Gorham St. Fairgrounds, Lowell, Mass., in summer of 1906 as noted balloonist Charles J. Glidden takes off. (Lowell Hist. Soc.)

### GLOBE PRIZE OF $10,000 — TO ENCOURAGE AVIATION

The *Globe* offered this prize for the fastest round-trip, 33-mile flight from Squantum Field, Quincy, to Boston Light. Claude Graham-White, pioneer English aviator, flew it Sept. 12, 1910, a feat hailed as "the longest flight over salt water in the United States."

*b*  White flies over Squantum Field.

*c*  Donor of prize, *Globe* publisher Gen. Chas. H. Taylor (*second from right*) with official group and Graham-White. (*second from left*)

*a*

b

c

*a*

*a*  New England's first tri-state flight was initiated by another $10,000 *Globe* prize and won Sept. 4, 1911 by Earle L. Ovington, Newton "birdman," who flew 160 miles, Boston-Nashua, N.H.-Worcester-Providence-Boston in 3 hours and 6 minutes in a 100 horse-power Bleriot monoplane. He was seen by 3 million en route, most seeing an airplane for the first time. (AP)

*b*  On the links of The Country Club in Brookline in 1913, Francis Ouimet of Wellesley won the playoff for the U.S. Open Golf Championship over two con-tenders. By his victory Ouimet, who would win the U.S. Amateur in 1914 and 1931, transformed the game from strictly a rich man's to anyone's sport. Ouimet and caddy. (The Country Club)

*c*  The Champs – The Red Sox, in a sensation-packed 10th inn-ing victory, became the world champions at then new Fenway Park Oct. 16, 1912 by defeating the New York Giants 3-2. Right fielder Harry Hooper, at bat, saved the game in the fifth inn-ing when he thwarted a sure Giant homer with a catch in far right field – the greatest of his career. (BPL)

*d*  Evangelist Rev. William Ashley "Billy" Sunday, ex-baseball pro, opened his 10-week revival Nov. 12, 1916 in his newly built Tabernacle – with its 40 or so entrances – on the old Huntington Avenue baseball grounds. His acrobatics and plain talk drew as many as 60,000 a day to watch him fight Beelzebub or "hit the sawdust-trail." Rev. Sunday "laying down the law to husbands."

*e*  Five-foot Hazel Hotchkiss Wightman won four U.S. Women's Singles tennis titles (the first in 1909) and eventually 45 titles in all. She won a senior crown when she was 68, coached at Brookline's Longwood Cricket Club into her late 80s. In 1919 she gave the world of tennis the Wightman Cup. (Mrs. William Wightman)

*b*

c

d

e

a

b

*a*  "Unsinkable" White Star liner *Titanic*, world's largest liner, took two dozen New Englanders to the bottom when she sank April 15, 1912 after hitting an iceberg off the Grand Banks, roughly 1000 miles east of Boston. Tragedy sketched by *Globe* artist from wireless reports.

*b*  Lawrence textile strike, Jan. 12, 1912, by 30,000 workers, over a pay cut resulting from a new state law reducing the work week to 54 hours, lasted two months with some rioting, window-smashing, clashes with police and encounters with militia bayonets. (Brown Brothers)

*c*  Just after noon Jan. 15, 1919 a 50-foot-high iron tank containing 2,300,000 gallons of molasses exploded, sending a 15-foot tidal wave across Commercial Street to the harbor in Boston's North End, drowning and killing 21 people, injuring 40, sweeping away six buildings.

*d*  Protesting suspension of 19 patrolmen for union activity, roughly three-quarters of Boston's police went on strike Sept. 9, 1919. Rowdies roamed the streets, smashing windows and looting, until volunteers and state militia restored order. A new force of 1100 recruits and 400 police who did not strike took over the city on Dec. 20 when the militia was withdrawn. Scene: State Guard arresting looters.

*c*

*d*

a

*a*   Eamonn de Valera, arriving June 28, 1919 at Boston's old South Station, was greeted by the largest Boston throng ever to welcome a foreign visitor. Next day thousands from all over New England crowded Fenway Park to hear him plead the cause of a free Ireland.

*b*   Nearly three years before the 19th Amendment giving women the right to vote, Gov. R. Livingston Beeckman placed Rhode Island among pioneer civil rights states by signing a law April 17, 1917 so Rhode Island women could vote in presidential elections. (RIHS)

*c*   President Woodrow Wilson, landing in Boston, Feb. 24, 1919, during a pause in the Peace Conference at Paris, got an ovation at old Mechanics Hall when he said a peace pact would be but "a scrap of paper" without a league of nations "to set up new standards of right in the world." Wilson motorcade passes the State House. (BPL)

*b*

*c*

*a*

*b*

*a*  Future "Sultan of Swat," George Herman "Babe" Ruth, at 18, joined the Boston Red Sox as a left-handed pitcher and outfielder, helped them win the pennant in 1918. He hit 29 four-baggers in 1919, hailed as a world record, but the needy Red Sox traded him to the N.Y. Yankees for $100,000. (Baseball Hall of Fame)

*b*  Clarence DeMarr of Melrose at the finish line in the annual Patriots' Day 26-mile marathon in 1923, his third victory. Between 1911 and 1930 he won it seven times, even in 1927 when the heat hit 85 degrees!

*c*  The first American to swim the English Channel was Henry F. Sullivan, 31, 5-foot-6½, 220 pounds, of Lowell's Catholic Young Men's Lyceum. On Aug. 5-6, 1923, he swam from Dover to Calais in 27 hours and 25 minutes after six earlier attempts going back to 1913. Scene: Sullivan at Calais after 1923 swim. (Sister Augusta Sullivan, SCN)

*d*  The Prince of Wales, later King and Duke of Windsor, with his host Bayard Tuckerman, Jr., (*left*) during brief visit to Hamilton, Mass., estate Oct. 23, 1924 for lunch, a drag hunt at the Myopia Hunt Club, followed by tea at the Tuckermans' and a dinner-dance.

c

d

*a*  Tighter pressure was put upon scofflaws, rumrunners and bootleggers when Dept. of Justice agents took over in 1929 from the Treasury Dept. An East Cambridge police raiding party pours illicit liquor down the sewer.

*b*  John Barleycorn's "funeral" was staged by Boston prohibitionists at the Morgan Memorial with the 18th Amendment's prohibition to take effect at midnight Jan. 16, 1920. Barleycorn's fans bid their "au revoir" at hotel and cafe revelries, "lugging the stuff" home in bags, autos and stomachs. (BPL)

*c*  Pilgrims' Tercentenary — President Warren G. Harding came on the presidential yacht *Mayflower* to Plymouth Aug. 1, 1921. He saw the pageant, rode in the parade, hailed the Pilgrims' spirit of liberty before 50,000 at Plymouth Rock and predicted a coming "brotherhood of nations." (Plymouth-Carver Regional High School)

*d*  President Calvin Coolidge, by the porch of his Vermont farmhouse Aug. 19, 1924 presents his great-great-grandfather's maple syrup bucket to automaker Henry Ford and friends on arrival from their vacation at Ford's Wayside Inn in Sudbury. *From left*: Inventor Harvey Firestone, Coolidge, Ford, Thomas A. Edison, Russell Firestone, Mrs. Coolidge and the President's father, Col. John Coolidge.

*a*

*b*

c

d

*"LONE EAGLE" CHARLES A. LINDBERGH, 25, FORMER AIRMAIL PILOT, BECAME AN INSTANT NATIONAL HERO MAY 20-21, 1927, WHEN HE WON A $25,000 PRIZE FOR THE FIRST NONSTOP NEW YORK-PARIS FLIGHT IN 33 HOURS AND 32 MINUTES.*

On his return, he toured 75 American cities traveling in the same "Spirit of St. Louis" with which he had conquered the Atlantic. In late July he flew to every New England state, landing on the sands of Old Orchard Beach, Maine, when fog kept his plane from Portland.

*a*  Lindbergh at Concord, N.H., July 23. (NHHS)

*b*  Lindbergh's welcome at Boston's State House was typical of his enthusiastic greeting throughout New England.

*a*

b

*a*  Sacco-Vanzetti –
Handcuffed and flanked by
guards, Bartolomeo Vanzetti,
left, and Nicola Sacco, right, on
their way to trial in Dedham
Courthouse May 31, 1921, for the
1920 South Braintree payroll
robbery in which two were
killed.

*b*  Funeral cortege for Sacco
and Vanzetti, witnessed by
200,000 spectators, moves
along Tremont Street, passing
Boston Common, a few days
after appeals and hunger strikes
failed and the two were electro-
cuted Aug. 23, 1927.

*c*  Pickwick Club Disaster –
Forty-four merrymakers were
killed and scores injured when
suddenly, near the end of a
Night-Before-the-Fourth dance,
the building – an old hotel on
Beach Street in Boston's
Chinatown – collapsed about
3 a.m. July 4, 1925.

*d*  Charles Ponzi, the "get-
rich-quick wizard," who had
promised to double any
investor's money in 90 days,
was sentenced July 11, 1925 as a
"common and notorious thief."
After serving four years in
Plymouth County Jail, Ponzi is
being deported on the *S.S.
Vulcania*.

*a*

*b*

c

d

*a*

*b*

**a** An ice storm Nov. 28-29, 1921 was called "the worst since the night the Portland went down." Freezing downpour shattered trees grotesquely, brought down miles of telephone and electric wires, crippled transportation. Worcester was among the hardest hit. Scene: Stafford Street, Worcester. (UPI)

**b** Vermont suffered its greatest disaster (84 killed) as New England was hit by torrents of rain that began Nov. 2, 1927 and dumped 7-11 inches within 45 hours, raising rivers to record heights. There were 105 dead, hundreds injured, hundreds of houses ruined, more than 15,000 people homeless. Bridges exceeding 1000 were demolished. Dams gave way by dozens. Scene: Otter Creek rampages past bridges in center of Rutland, Vt. (AP)

**c** Thirty-four sailors died on the S-4 when the submarine was struck by the Coast Guard cutter *Paulding* on an anti-rum-running run off Provincetown Dec. 17, 1927 and sank in 100 feet of water. Eight sailors, trapped in the forward torpedo room, tapped out appeals — 'Please hurry!' — for four days before dying. S-4, raised three months later, is towed to Boston. (Navy Dept.)

**d** A seemingly minor fire on a bridge over the Nashua River on May 4, 1930 was spread by stiff winds into the city of Nashua, N.H., destroying 260 dwellings, factories, churches, schools, leaving 1200 homeless in what Gov. Charles W. Tobey called the state's greatest loss by fire. (Nashua Public Library)

c

d

a

b

*a* "East Side, West Side" – New York Gov. Alfred "Al" Smith drew tremendous, wildly cheering crowds Oct. 24-25 in Massachusetts and Rhode Island in his 1928 presidential campaign against Herbert Hoover. Smith waves his ever-present brown derby. (BPL)

*b* "Lady Lindy" – After three women lost their lives in the attempt, Amelia Earhart, 29, a social worker at Boston's Dennison House, became the first woman to fly across the Atlantic. Battling rain and gale winds, Miss Earhart flew as co-pilot in 3-motored monoplane "Friendship" June 17-18, 1928 from Newfoundland to Wales.

*c* Back from South Pole, Commander Richard E. Byrd was given a tremendous home-town welcome in Boston June 28, 1930 in tribute to his being the first man to fly over both the North and South Poles. He fought four-mile heights and glacier winds in his monoplane to reach the South Pole Nov. 29, 1929.

*c*

## EMINENT IN NEW ENGLAND

*a*   Boston Mayor John F. "Honey Fitz" Fitzgerald, grandfather of his namesake, President John F. Kennedy. Wearing velvet collar and derby, for many years the required attire for Boston politicians, he is about to step into his official automobile outside the City Hall in 1910.

*b*   Mrs. John L. "Jack" Gardner (1840-1924), wealthy New York socialite who married a wealthy Boston banker, enjoyed flaunting her eccentric ways on proper Boston society. She was, though, an impeccable art connoisseur and willed to the public her magnificent, reassembled Italian palace, the present Isabella Stewart Gardner Museum, in which she collected world treasured Renaissance sculpture and furnishings as well as masterpieces of Raphael, Titian and Rembrandt.

*c*   Gen. John J. Pershing (1860-1948). A West Point graduate, Pershing rose from our late Indian campaigns in the West to become Commander-in-Chief of the American Expeditionary Force in Europe in World War I. He is pictured here in the 1920 commencement procession at Harvard where he received an honorary degree.

*d*   Maxfield Parrish (1870-1966), painter and illustrator, did many famous magazine covers in the opening decades of the Twentieth Century. His was a long New England background, from painting his "Old King Cole" when 19 years old to "Getting Away from it All" when he was 91. (Maxfield Parrish, Jr.)

*e*   Eugene O'Neill (1888-1953). Flunked out of Princeton, young O'Neill became a common sailor and waterfront drifter, then blossomed as actor and playwright in Provincetown, Cape Cod. Several of his famous plays are "Long Day's Journey into Night," "Strange Interlude," and "The Iceman Cometh," with many characters drawn from his own experiences.

*a*

*b*

*c*

*f*    John Dos Passos (1896-1970), who lived and wrote many years on Cape Cod, brought new realism and immediacy to his novels of Twentieth Century life with devices he called "The Camera Eye" and "News Reel." Among his novels are *Three Soldiers*, with many of his World War I experiences, and the *U.S.A.* trilogy covering three decades of American life.

*g*    Amy Lowell (1874-1925), poet and pioneer in free verse, gave to the public her exhaustive biography and manuscript collection — the world's best — of a great English poet she admired, John Keats. "Patterns," her most celebrated poem, strains against the strange restrictions of life. She is shown here in her Brookline, Mass. home.

*d*

*e*

*f*

*g*

**a**  "Banned in Boston" – Eugene O'Neill's Pulitzer Prize 9-act play "Strange Interlude," banned by Boston's Mayor Malcolm "Mal" Nichols as "not a fit spectacle for the public," opened Sept. 30, 1929 on schedule before a capacity audience in Quincy's old Quincy Theatre. Opening scene of this Theater Guild production starring Judith Anderson. (New York Public Library)

**b**  Britain's Sir Thomas Lipton became a preeminent winner in sportsmanship when he and his boat *Shamrock V* lost his fifth attempt to win the American Cup trophy in 1930 that he had started seeking back in 1899. Admiring American yachtsmen gave Sir Thomas a gold cup for being "the world's best loser."

**c**  Eddie Shore, often called the "Babe Ruth" of hockey, starred in Boston Bruins' winning the Stanley Cup 1929-1930. Shore was the first defenseman to leave the blue line and race the rink's length to score. A rough player, he had 100 stitches in his 20-year career.

**d**  George Owen of Milton, nine-letter man at Harvard in three sports, brought the carriage trade to Boston Garden hockey when he joined the Bruins in 1928. Fast skater with a fine wrist shot, Owen was hailed as the greatest college hockey player since legendary Hobey Baker of Princeton.

**e**  Jack Sharkey, the "Boston Gob," squire of Chestnut Hill (later of Epping, N.H.), got his start boxing in the navy, won the world title June 21, 1932, in a 15-round decision over Max Schmeling. Sharkey was the only champ to fight both Jack Dempsey and Joe Louis. (AP)

*a*

*b*

c

d

e

**a**    Boston's "vastest" throngs packed windows, sidewalks and streets to bring its 300th anniversary celebration to a close Sept. 17, 1930 with a parade of 50,000 marchers. Boston's Mayor James M. Curley and His Worship the Mayor of Boston, England, from the reviewing stand in front of city hall, watch the parade go up School Street.

**b**    Depths of Depression — Woe-etched faces of unemployed men in 1930. Lineups — for jobs, soup kitchens or help — were commonplace after the 1929 Stock Market crash and the onset of America's worst-ever economic recession. (AP)

**c**    A "New Deal" for America was pledged by Franklin D. Roosevelt. Campaigning in Boston Oct. 31, 1932 before a wildly enthusiastic audience that filled old Boston Arena, FDR got ovation on ovation as he assailed fear and pledged warfare against the Depression and all its evils.

b

c

# News Photos

# 1933—1952

## New Deal Era

"My friends!"

The vibrance with which new President Franklin D. Roosevelt uttered those words, the sincerity, and, too, the courage of this man who had bravely overcome but yet bore the ravages of polio – all brought new heart to a nation stricken by the worst depression in our annals. All felt they could genuinely rely on his assurance:

"We have nothing to fear but fear itself."

Once again the bands could convincingly play his campaign tune: "Happy days are here again!"

FDR would be re-elected in a sweep, and go on to re-election to a third and fourth term, only President in America's history to be given more than two terms by the voters. The New Deal would continue under President Harry S. Truman until the election of General Dwight D. Eisenhower in 1952 brought two decades of Democratic rule to an end.

This New Deal period is remembered not just for its long overdue social reforms but for epochal events: World War II and the advent of the Atomic Age. Lightning advances in modern weaponry are underscored by the appearance of the A-bomb in 1945 and a short seven years later an H-bomb touched off in the Pacific testing ground at Eniwetok Atoll.

For most Americans who lived in the New Deal era two events have remained personally memorable. Most had been so impressed that they could recall precisely where they were – even remember the time of day – when these two events happened: news that Pearl Harbor had been attacked and the day that FDR died at Warm Springs, Ga.

For news photography the New Deal era brought breakthroughs. Camera work got new recognition with the appointment of a photography editor in 1937, the *Globe*'s Lucien Thayer. Photographers began to receive picture credits and pictures received a greater role in layout. It was in this era that color photography made great technical advances. This had been long in coming, for even back in 1827 Louis Daguerre made experiments – without success – to obtain color pictures; and we had known from British experiments in 1861 that any color could be created by mixing three primary colors, red, blue and green, the way modern presses print color. Difficulties of color registration and costs inhibited extensive use.

Black and white photography saw refinements in film, especially its speed, and in cameras that produced increasingly superior photos. Pictures were made widely that once seemed far beyond any camera's capability. The bitter effects of the depression are incised on the faces of the unemployed men on page 71 as is the torment of great responsibility on the face of FDR with only a few weeks of life left for him, in the likeness on page 88.

The matchless advantage of fast film – and quick action by the photographer – can be enjoyed in the spectacular picture, page 83, showing the bow of the ill-fated submarine *Squalus* suddenly popping above the surface and sinking again almost immediately.

Photos such as these are a fulfillment of all the promise inherent in the camera at its birth.

Few newspaper libraries ("morgues," newsmen call them) have the facilities to retain all the photos that their photographers make over the years. To reproduce news photos in newspaper rotogravure or in this book, the originals or photographic copies are necessary. Old copies of newspapers or microfilm of past newspapers is inadequate. The search for missing photographs led to many places, among them the Boston Public Library.

Unhappily, the search was not always fruitful. Countless news photos have disappeared and exist only in old newspapers or newspaper microfilm. This prompted a question. Of all the great treasures in a great library, which, in case of a catastrophe like a fire, would a librarian seek to save?

"That's easy," replied the Boston librarian. "The newspapers or microfilm. They contain the best idea we have of the past. Everything else is replaceable."

*Left*: On eve of America's entry into World War II, President Roosevelt toured the nation on military preparedness inspection trips. Sailors watched from destroyer decks at old Charlestown Navy Yard Aug. 10, 1940. "We are really getting into our stride," said smiling FDR. (*Globe*/Paul Maguire)

*Right*: Ex-mayor John F. ("Honey Fitz") Fitzgerald, on his 81st birthday Feb. 11, 1944, puts arm around his namesake grandson, Lt. John Fitzgerald Kennedy just back from the Pacific where the future president was severely wounded and won honors in PT boat warfare. (*Globe*/Paul Maguire)

*a*    John Barleycorn's return – There was merriment, as in this barroom scene, but there was also a hampering shortage of licenses and supplies as liquor made a legal reappearance after 14 years of repeal when Utah, at 5:31 p.m. eastern time Dec. 5, 1933 became the 36th state to approve (and make effective) the 21st repeal amendment.

*THE FIRESIDE CHATS – FDR WAS SWEPT INTO THE WHITE HOUSE IN 1932 ELECTION BY A TIDAL WAVE OF VOTES, CARRYING ALL BUT SIX STATES.*

He kept in close contact with the voters in radio talks from his White House office and pressed upon Congress anti-depression programs that would become collectively the "New Deal."

*b*    In his first Fireside Chat on March 12, 1933 FDR ended a four-day Bank Holiday that he had imposed to prevent gold, silver and currency from fleeing abroad or being hoarded, and explained why our banking system was now sound. (Franklin D. Roosevelt Library)

*c*    Civilian Conservation Corps, which provided jobs for some three million unemployed, unmarried men 17 to 23 years of age, was one of several "alphabet" agencies – PWA, WPA, NRA, etc. – that FDR created to fight Depression. Scene: CCC men at work in New Hampshire forest.

*a*

*b*

c

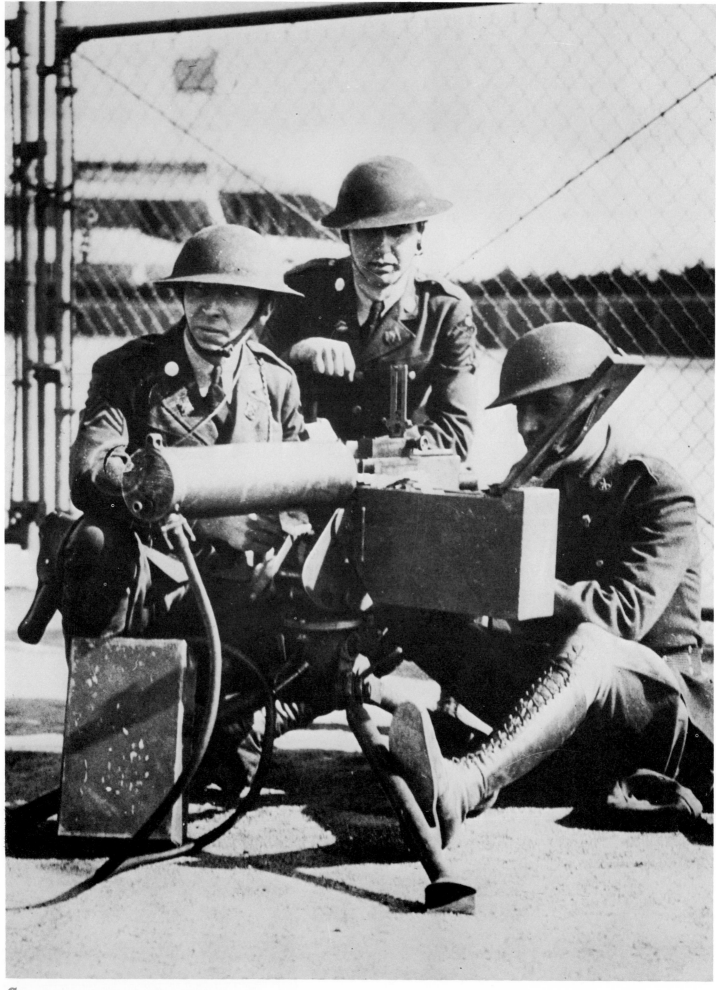

*a*

*a*   Determined to remove sportsman Walter E. O'Hara as director of Narragansett race track in Pawtucket, R.I., Gov. Robert E. Quinn declared martial law and had 300 R.I. National Guardsmen mount machine guns at the track entrances Oct. 18, 1937, shutting off the fall race meet. (UPI)

*b*   The month-long sensational trial of Jessie B. Costello, 30, charged with the poison murder of her husband, Peabody, Mass., fire chief, brought her freedom – and a return to her three children – when the jury, after brief deliberation Aug. 15, 1933 proclaimed her not guilty. Mrs. Costello being conducted from jail two hours before verdict. (AP)

*c*   For three months the brothers (*l-r*) Irving Millen, 21, and Murton, 24, of Roxbury and Abraham Faber, 25, of Dorchester, M.I.T. honor graduate, terrorized eastern Massachusetts with a series of robberies in which they killed four men and wounded three. Early June 7, 1935 all three were executed after the state's longest (eight weeks') capital trial. (AP)

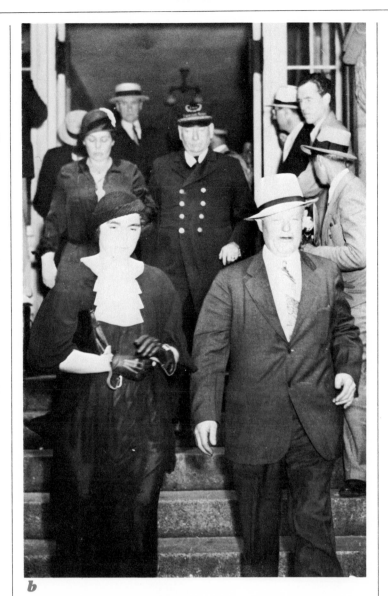

*b*

*c*

a

b

c

*a* Charles Christopher "Chuckin' Charlie" O'Rourke, in the most famous of Boston College gridiron victories, passed and ran the Eagles to a last-minute triumph over Tennessee in a Sugar Bowl classic in New Orleans Jan. 1, 1941. For O'Rourke it won a niche in college football's Hall of Fame.

*b* Tennis star Sarah Palfrey of Brookline, 5 feet 3, who became national junior champ at 14, went on to win the singles crown in 1941 and again in 1945 plus some 30 other national titles.

*c* First ski tow in U.S. got going in Jan. 1934 on farmer Gilbert's Hill in Woodstock, Vt., its 500 feet of rope lines powered by an old Ford tractor. An improvisation of three college boys, the contraption led on to T-bars, J-bars and chair-lifts that have made skiing thrive in Vermont. (Woodstock Hist. Soc.)

*d* Valentine's Day storm— One way to get up Park Street hill to the State House when the 1940 snowfall and gale brought transportation to a standstill.

*d*

a

***a*** Harvard, America's oldest university, concluded its tercentenary with fireworks on the Charles River, bestowal of degrees on world scholars and alumnus President Franklin D. Roosevelt's address Sept. 18, 1936 to 15,000 gathered in the Yard. Brilliant rocket burst lights up riverside dorms and a float on which the Harvard band was playing. (Harvard Archives)

***b*** The big $3 million bridges spanning Cape Cod Canal were dedicated by Gov. James M. Curley Aug. 15, 1935 as 30,000 spectators lined the banks and a naval parade moved through the seven-mile canal. Bourne Bridge, 285 feet above sea level, nears completion.

***c*** New Haven's 20-foot birthday cake with 300 candles for its Tercentenary was lighted on Central Green May 28, 1938 and 20,000 marched to open two weeks of festivities, an exposition and spectacle with a cast of 4000. Parade moves along Chapel Street. (New Haven Colony Historical Society)

b

*a*

*b*

## HURRICANE OF 1938 —

Wind gusts at an incredible 186 mph, tidal waves in Buzzards Bay, a hurricane that lashed all New England but raced with screaming devastation up the Connecticut Valley left 588 dead or missing, thousands injured, 18,731 buildings destroyed and damage estimated at $300 million. Called the worst since the gale of 1815, the hurricane swept away bridges, crippled transportation and communication.

*a*   Water in front of the City Hall in Providence, R.I., reached a record 6 feet 2 inches deep. (RIHS)

*b*   Melting upland snow and ice and cloudbursts of rain in the White Mountains swelled New England rivers to record heights, sent them rampaging March 18-20, 1936, sweeping away bridges, dams, and highways. Flooding was widespread. Warning kept down the loss of life but tens of thousands were left homeless. Hartford was like an inland sea as the Connecticut reached an all-time high of 37.6 feet. (CHS)

*c*   Carrying 26 entombed sailors, the bow of the ill-starred submarine *Squalus* surfaces for 10 seconds July 13, 1939 and sinks again 240 feet to ocean floor during a mishap in salvage operations off Isle of Shoals, N.H. A new diving bell rescued 33 other sailors when the *Squalus* sank during test dives May 23, 1939. (*Globe*/James A. Jones)

*d*   Cocoanut Grove fire — Nearly 1000 merrymakers, many of them servicemen, were crowded into the Boston nightclub when a flash fire late on Nov. 28, 1942, started a stampede in which victims were trampled, crushed, burned or killed by fumes. Boston's worst tragedy resulted in 490 killed, 166 injured. (Bill Noonan)

*c*

*d*

*a*

*b*

*a*    Gigantic campaign windup rally for FDR at the Boston Garden Oct. 31, 1940.

*b*    FDR, son Elliott beside him, waves to Garden throng.

*c*    "Day that will live in infamy" – Army recruiters in Boston gather around radio to hear the President's call to Congress to declare war on Japan immediately after the sneak attack on Pearl Harbor, Dec. 7, 1941.

*d*    Eleanor Roosevelt, tireless traveler and "eyes and ears of the President," told debs at International Students gathering April 10, 1942 in Boston's Hotel Vendome that the nation's war production could use their volunteer help in factories. Mrs. Roosevelt's relaxation: ever-present knitting.

*e*    In America for a war conference with FDR, Sir Winston Churchill made a secret trip Sept. 6, 1943 to Cambridge to receive an honorary degree and warn that the war was entering its "most severe and costly phase." Churchill outside Harvard's Memorial Chapel. (AP)

c

d

e

a

b

**a**   After a six weeks' impeachment trial – first in Massachusetts in 120 years – Executive Councilor Daniel H. Coakley on Oct. 3, 1941 was ousted by the State Senate for misconduct on pardons and was barred from any public office. Coakley (*right*) with his chief counsel William H. Lewis in the Senate chamber.

**b**   Bretton Woods Conference – At President Roosevelt's invitation, financial experts from 44 nations met in New Hampshire July 1, 1944 for three weeks to establish world banks to stabilize international exchange and aid trade revival after World War II. Treasury Secretary Henry Morgenthau opens conference. (UPI)

**c**   Fire spreading like lightning through the big tent of the Ringling Brothers and Barnum and Bailey Circus during the matinee in Hartford, Conn., July 6, 1944 spurred a stampede for exits that caused 169 deaths – most of them of children – and injured 682. (Hartford Courant)

c

*a*   Fourth Term — With World War II victory still a half-year away, FDR came to Fenway Park Nov. 4, 1944 for his campaign wind-up speech in which he thrilled an overflow crowd with an attack on his rival, N.Y. Gov. Thomas E. Dewey. Victory on the Western Front was less than a month away when FDR died April 12, 1945.

*b*   Gen. George S. Patton Jr., 60, of Hamilton, Mass., a genius in tank warfare who led the 3rd Army from the Normandy Beaches right across the Rhine and earned the nickname "Old Blood and Guts," died at Heidelberg Dec. 21, 1945 from injuries suffered in an army automobile crash.

*c*   U.S. Senator Henry Cabot Lodge, at 42, became the first Senator since Civil War days to seek active duty when, resuming his rank of Army captain, he told his Senate colleagues Feb. 4, 1944 he was resigning and headed for the battlefront where he won six battle stars and promotion. Lodge in Germany.

*d*   Victory in Europe (VE) Day May 7, 1945, has young people dancing near Boston's Liberty Square, on Milk and Kilby streets, showered gaily with torn paper, to celebrate the end of World War II in Europe. (BPL)

*e*   Flying directly from Europe where he led the Allied armies that defeated Hitler, Gen. Dwight D. Eisenhower was given a triumphant welcome in Boston's Armistice Day parade Nov. 11, 1945. "Ike" rides with his wife, Mamie, and Gov. Maurice J. Tobin.

*a*

*b*

*c*

d

e

***a*** Wartime price controls on meat were ended by President Harry Truman on Oct. 15, 1946 as shoppers stood in long lines to get any meat at all. Price controls were retained on wages and scarce items like automobiles and household appliances. Line for poultry formed at 3 a.m. on Fulton Place in Boston's North End.

***b*** Marshall Plan—Secretary of State George C. Marshall, soldier and statesman, was given an honorary degree at Harvard's Commencement June 5, 1947 and that day gave a speech unveiling a plan to prevent postwar chaos in Europe. Marshall accepts award from university marshal Reginald Fitz as Gen. Omar Bradley, seated, applauds.

***a***

***b***

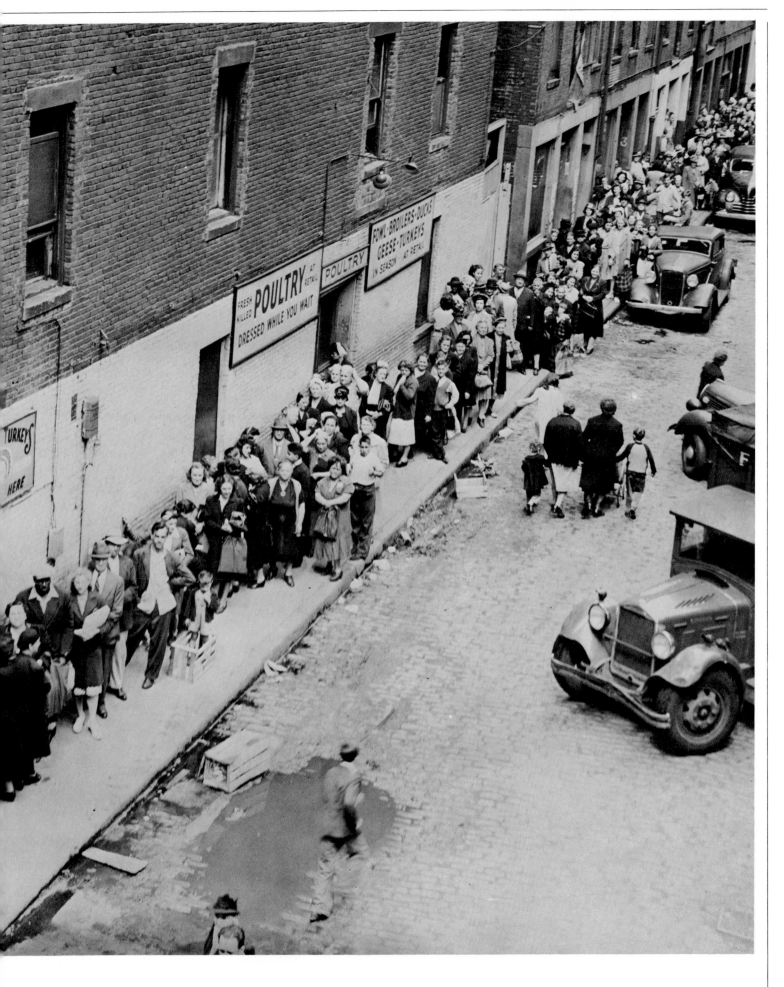

a

b

## EMINENT IN NEW ENGLAND

***a***    Robert Frost (1875-1963), mill-worker, teacher, chicken and dirt farmer, won Pulitzer Prizes with his poetic reflections on New England life and became the nation's poet laureate with his "Gift Outright," recited in 1961 at the Kennedy inaugural in Washington, D.C.

***b***    Walter Gropius (1883-1969), founded the international style of modern architecture with a glass-walled German shoe factory in 1911. He created the famous German Bauhaus School of Design at Weimar, was driven out by Hitler and became head of architecture at Harvard's Graduate School. Here Gropius checks his model for the law school dormitories.

***c***    Sergei Koussevitzky (1874-1951) was born in Russia where he directed the Moscow Symphony and Grand Opera under the last czars. After the October Revolution he became a leader in Europe's musical world, and in 1924, conductor of the Boston Symphony Orchestra. Leading its musicians in summer concerts there, he advanced the Berkshire Music Center, named Tanglewood in 1937.

***d***    Fred Allen (1894-1956), stage name of Cambridge-born John F. Sullivan, who along with his wife Portland Hoffa was radio's deadpan comedian in the 1930's and 40's. Allen acted earlier in vaudeville, musical comedy and movies. For radio fans he created "Allen's Alley" and several notable characters, including Senator Claghorn, Mrs. Nussbaum and Titus Moody.

***e***    Bette Davis, born 1908 in Lowell, Mass., was for years a leading player in stock, on Broadway and then films in 1931. Her 1934 portrayal of Mildred in Somerset Maugham's *Of Human Bondage* made her a star. She has won many Academy Awards. Some of her great roles were in *The Private Lives of Elizabeth and Essex, The Little Foxes, All About Eve* and *Hush, Hush Sweet Charlotte.*

c

d

e

*a*

**a**   Mayor James M. Curley, 72, ex-governor, ex-congressman, four times Boston's mayor, was sent to the Danbury, Conn., prison June 26, 1947 to serve 6-18 months for mail fraud but resumed his mayoral duties Nov. 26 when pardoned by President Truman. (AP)

**b**   Snowiest Winter on record, 1947-48 – Biggest storm brought a 15-inch snowfall in 20 hours a day after Christmas, 1947, paralyzing most New England communities. Scene: Howard Street near railroad station in downtown Framingham as it looked on Dec. 27. By March, 1948, intown Boston's 1915 record of 79.2 inches of winter snow was exceeded by 10 inches.

**c**   Strong winds spread dozens of fires through New England's drought-stricken forests Oct. 21-25, 1947, engulfing communities and killing 18 persons. Maine was hardest hit with 1056 houses burned, 6000 persons homeless. Flames swept Mt. Desert Island, leaving a third of fashionable Bar Harbor, Maine, hotels, mansions and houses in ashes. (Coast Guard air photo – UPI)

**b**

**c**

*a*   "Perambulating Parson" – Rev. Gilbert L. "Gil" Dodds competed for Boston Athletic Assn. in early 1940s, got a divinity degree in 1945, set world record of 4:05.3 for indoor mile run at Millrose Games in 1948. (AP)

*b*   Jubilant Boston Braves players celebrate their first pennant in 34 years with manager Billy Southworth hoisted on the shoulders of Red Barrett, left, and Sibby Sisti after beating the Giants 3-to-2 at old Braves Field Sept. 26, 1948.

*c*   Rocky Marciano, born in Brockton, got his start in boxing by beating a bully in a World War II army camp. On Sept. 23, 1952 he won the world championship with a KO of Jersey Joe Walcott in the 13th round, defended his title six times, retired undefeated in 1956. Marciano just after beating Walcott. (AP)

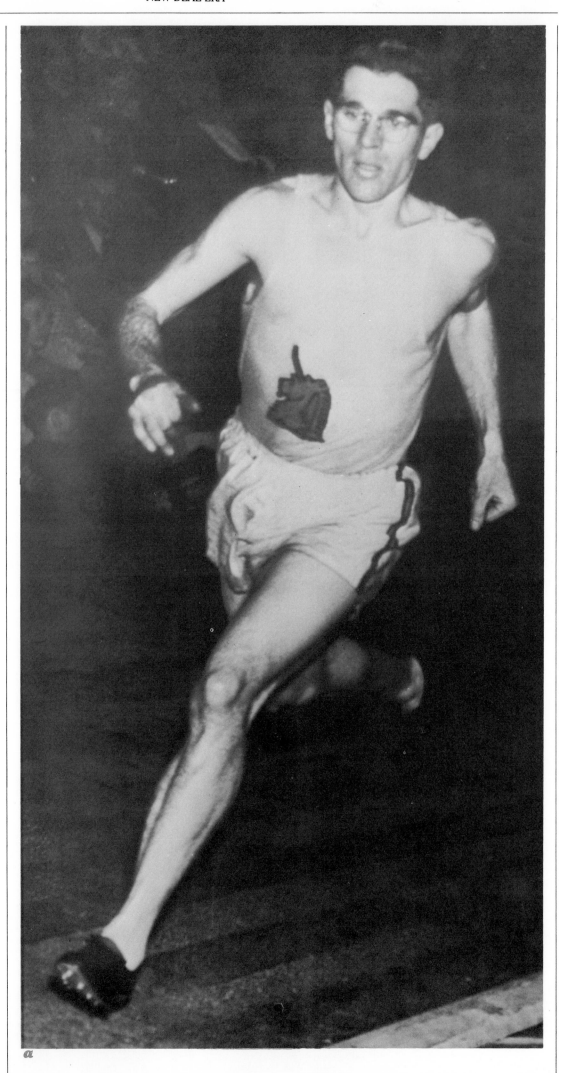

*a*

b

c

*a*

*a*  On the final days of the 1948 presidential election upset that would have the political prophets committing "Dewey-cide," smiling President Harry S. Truman told huge outpourings of voters that Gov. Dewey was "following me around, and that's where he'll be on election day." Underdog Truman plays piano during campaign swing through Hartford. (*Globe*/Charles McCormick)

*b*  "Eolia," 235-acre seaside estate with 42-room mansion at Waterford, Conn., was given June, 1950 to the public by the widow of Edward S. Harkness as part of $60 million bequests to charity. Financeer Harkness also made possible the multi-million-dollar house plans at both Harvard and Yale.

*c*  Waltham Watch plant, oldest in the nation (1854) and once the largest precision watchmaker in the world, was forced to close its doors Feb. 3, 1950, putting 2300 employees out of work, when unable to obtain sufficient capital to operate.

b

c

a

b

*a*   Dr. Herman N. Sander, 42-year-old country doctor, was found not guilty March 9, 1950 after a three-weeks' jury trial in Manchester, N.H., for allegedly murdering a 59-year-old cancer-doomed woman by injecting air into her veins. Dr. and Mrs. Sander leaving courtroom after verdict. (UPI)

*b*   Biggest armed car robbery – Three robbers within two minutes took $681,000 from a U.S. Trucking Corp. armored car parked in Danvers Square on March 25, 1952, while its guards were taking a coffee break. Scene: Reenactment for Federal jury that, on April 14, 1954 set free a Wollaston suspect who two months later was mysteriously, fatally shot in Boston's Franklin Park.

### THE FBI BROKE THE JAN. 17, 1950 BRINK'S ROBBERY IN BOSTON'S NORTH END –

$1,219,000 was stolen – with the announcement Dec. 18, 1952 that Joseph J. "Specs" O'Keefe, 44, was a participant and $60,000 loot had been found in his garage in Stoughton. Eight other robbers were sentenced to life terms.

*c*   Brink's counting room and looted cash vault on Prince Street, North End. Leaving vault is Thomas B. Lloyd, left, cashier-in-charge at time of holdup. (AP)

*d*   "Specs" O'Keefe, middle, with deputy sheriffs.

MONEY BAGS DISREGARDED BY HOLDUP MEN

CAP LEFT BEHIND

*c*

*d*

***a***    President Truman came to Groton, Conn., June 14, 1952 for the keel-laying ceremony of America's pioneer submarine *USS Nautilus* and warned national defense cannot be obtained "at cut-rate, bargain-counter prices."

***b***    "Mr. Speaker!"—Leaders in their respective parties in 1951, Democrat John W. McCormack (left) and Republican Joseph W. Martin Jr., started their public lives in the Bay State Legislature, went to Congress in the early 1920s, served as their party floor leaders for two decades and each later became Speaker of the House.

***c***    Gen. Eisenhower, who began his White House campaign in New England on March 11 by sweeping New Hampshire's first-in-the-nation primaries, did a whirlwind windup campaign swing through Boston on Nov. 4, 1952, election eve; with a final address before an overflow crowd in Boston Garden. Scene: Tremont Street at Park Street. (*Globe*/Paul Maguire)

*a*

*b*

c

# News Photos

# 1953–1978

## War and Protest

The father of photography, Louis Daguerre, a sort of magician himself, would have called the photographic equipment of these times sheer magic:

Edwin H. Land's Polaroid and its instant photographs. Instant color, too.

And instant movies!

Sophisticated filters and lenses.

Portable devices so a news cameraman can hook into a telephone system anywhere and transmit back to the office.

Pictures sent to the earth from the moon – and even from the planets!

Action, automatic enlivener of any photograph, was widespread in these years of seemingly interminable war, protests of every variety against war, desperate demands for equal civil rights for all Americans, confrontations, street demonstrations, marches and violence:

June 11, 1963 – By order of President Kennedy, Federal troops turn aside Alabama Gov. George C. Wallace and his state troopers to enroll two 20-year-old black students at the University of Alabama.

Aug. 28, 1963 – Thousands of New Englanders by busload join 210,000 singing, praying civil rights demonstraters at the Lincoln Memorial, Washington, D.C. "Jim Crow must Go!"

March 9, 1965 – Boston Unitarian Universalist clergyman Rev. James J. Reeb, 38, dies from clubbing during civil rights demonstration at Selma, Ala.

March 21-25, 1965 – Fifty-thousand, joined by great numbers from New England, climax the 54-mile "Freedom Now!" march from Selma to Montgomery, Ala., where Gov. Wallace in his state house turned aside the petition of Rev. Dr. Martin Luther King, Jr., asking that Alabama extend to blacks the right to vote.

Oct. 15, 1969 – Students' campus protests against draft and R.O.T.C. reached a summit with millions marking Vietnam Moratorium Day nation-wide, San Francisco to Washington, D.C., appealing for an end of the war "Now!" Largest outpouring was Boston's 100,000 on the Common.

Contrasts in this period seemed the nadir and apex of national pride:

Richard M. Nixon, to avoid impeachment, becoming on Aug. 7, 1974, the first American president to resign – and, the apex, Americans becoming the first mortals to land on the moon's "magnificent desolation" July 20, 1969.

In an age of once incredible space travel it is fascinating to recall that when the Boston Globe began publication back in the early 1870's, a reporter rushing to an assignment would take a herdic. Herdic? This was a two-wheel, rear entry, side seat, horse-drawn cab.

Herdics have vanished as have other newspaper wonders like the old rotary press with which the Globe began. It could print what seemed an amazing 5000 eight-page newspapers in an hour. A few years later, and in a new building, the Globe installed New England's first quadruple press. Then, on its silver anniversary, it began using New England's first sextuple press, one capable of printing 72,000 newspapers an hour.

This tradition of the Globe to keep pace with innovations – and its steady growth to New England's largest newspaper – led to the Globe moving on May 11, 1958 to its newest and present plant, one of the most modern in the world.

In the two decades since that day, growth and innovations have continued. One example, type setting:

Type from old hand-type cases was the rule when the Globe began although very shortly thereafter this technique was put in limbo by arrival of the "wonderful linotype machine." For generations daily newspaper printing without linotype machines seemed impossible. But now, this technique has gone the way of the hand-set type.

Photography, in combination with electronics and the computer, has put an end to the reign of the linotype machine. Type instead is now being set by photography. Indeed, this very year even the writing of stories is being shifted from typewriter copy paper to electronic screens – and thence to photographically sensitized plates for printing.

For newspaper readers, however, the greatest change of all over the years was the coming of news photos. When well done, they make any printed page abound with life.

Left: Boston Common draws largest of the coast-to-coast demonstrations on Moratorium Day Oct. 15, 1969 as 100,000 Greater Bostonians demand an end to the "cruel and futile war in Vietnam." (Globe/Harry Holbrook)

Right: Rev. Martin Luther King in Roxbury April 23, 1965 to lead march to Boston Freedom Rally against "discrimination and to help make war on poverty." (Globe/Paul Connell)

a

b

*a*  New England's worst tornado cut a 25-mile, zigzag path through Worcester and seven nearby towns soon after 5 p.m. June 9, 1953, killing 98 (most of them in Worcester), injuring 2300, razing 1000 buildings, leaving 10,000 homeless.

*b*  Four mysterious explosions killed 36, wounded 25 aboard the huge *USS Leyte,* 856-foot aircraft carrier, Oct. 16, 1953 while moored for repair at the South Boston Naval Shipyard Annex. Blasts made a shambles of the port catapult room four decks below the flight deck. Firefighters fought three hours to quell the blaze.

*THREE HURRICANES, IN QUICK SUCCESSION, ROARED TOWARD NEW ENGLAND IN THE FALL OF 1954.*

Carol, with gusts beyond 100 mph, struck Aug. 31, leaving 63 dead, 1000 injured, 50,000 homes damaged. The coast was strewn with wrecked boats and yachts. The fierce wind toppled the steeple of Old North Church. Edna, its gusts up to 80 mph, unexpectedly veered seaward Sept. 11 but still swept the coastal area, particularly in eastern Maine, leaving 23 dead. On Oct. 15, Hazel, with 60-mile winds, suddenly veered westward, leaving only one man dead in New England, but more than 100 dead in its path.

*c*  Carol-caused wreckage at Menemsha, Martha's Vineyard. (AP)

c

***a*** Jacqueline Lee Bouvier, 24, and newly elected U.S. Senator John F. Kennedy were married by Archbishop Richard J. Cushing at St. Mary's Church, Newport, R.I., Sept. 12, 1953. Buffet and dancing for 1400 guests followed at the estate of the bride's family, Hammersmith Farm, overlooking Narragansett Bay. Scene: The smiling couple cut the wedding cake with best man Robert F. Kennedy all smiles, too.

***b*** U.S. Senate's "grand old man" – Colleagues June 17, 1956 honor Rhode Island Senator Theodore F. Green, (center) on becoming, at 88, the oldest man ever to serve in Congress. Twice governor of his state, Green was three times reelected to the Senate and retired in 1961 when he was 93. R.I. colleague John O. Pastore (left) and Vermont's George Aiken. (RIHS)

***c*** Tenley Albright Gardiner of Newton Center won the Eastern juvenile figure skating crown when she was 11, was five times U.S. champion and, at 21, became Olympic champion at the 1956 games. (AP)

***d*** The "king of figure skaters," Richard Totten "Dick" Button, 5 feet 10, 175 pounds, while at Harvard and Harvard Law School, 1948-55, won two Olympic gold medals and in 1952 made a still unequalled grand slam, winning the U.S., European, World and Olympic championships at age 22.

***e*** Ski Queen, Andrea "Andy" Mead Lawrence, 20, Vermont-born, scored double gold medal victories in ski events at the 1952 Winter Olympics. Famous for superb control, she won a long string of titles. Scene: "Andy" at Stowe, Vt., March 18, 1955 for American International Ski Races.

***a***

***b***

c

d

e

*a*    Ike's heart attack—Dr. Paul Dudley White, 69, for years chief of heart service at Mass. General Hospital, flew to the summer White House in Denver for consultation when President Eisenhower was stricken Sept. 24, 1955. Press Secretary Jim Hagerty, Dr. White on way to report on Ike's condition. (UPI)

*b*    Ike's top aide quits—Presidential Assistant Sherman Adams, ex-governor of New Hampshire, resigned from the White House Sept. 22, 1958 charging on nationwide TV that the Congressional probe into his taking gifts was a smear campaign. (AP)

*c*    Luxury liner *Andrea Doria,* inbound from Europe, sank 45 miles southeast of Nantucket July 26, 1956, 11 hours after a collision with the outbound liner *SS Stockholm* in a dense fog. Lifeboats of rescue ships took off most of the 1692 passengers and crew. There were 50 killed and missing, some 200 injured. (AP)

*d*    Hartford's cathedral, old St. Joseph's, a brownstone structure built in 1892 and Connecticut's largest church, was destroyed by a spectacular fire detected during the early Mass on Dec. 31, 1956. Ten firemen were injured. (CHS)

*a*

*b*

c

d

a

b

*a*   John F. Kennedy, 43, takes oath as President on chilly Jan. 20, 1961 in presence of ex-Presidents Truman and Eisenhower. Poet Frost recited a poem, Cardinal Cushing offered a blessing and smoke from a short circuit alarmed the nation. Kennedy urged both sides in the Cold War "begin anew a quest for peace." (*Globe*/Harry Holbrook)

*b*   Gen. Taylor's last surviving child, Mrs. Matthew G. Armstrong, on May 11, 1958 starts new presses rolling in the *Globe*'s new plant with her nephew, then Publisher William Davis Taylor and his son, William O. Taylor II, current publisher, standing by.

*c*   "What a beautiful view!" radioed back America's first man in space, Astronaut Alan B. Shepard, 37, of Derry, N.H. who was sent aloft in a space capsule at Cape Canaveral, May 5, 1961 and traveled for 16 minutes at speeds as high as 5100 mph. On return Navy Cmdr. Shepard exclaimed, "Boy, what a ride!"

*d*   Vermont's 1st Democratic governor in more than a century, Philip H. Hoff takes the oath of office in January, 1963, ending Republican Party's domination of Vermont's political life. Gov. Hoff was re-elected in 1964 and 1966. (*Barre-Montpelier Times Argus*)

c

d

*a*

## PRESIDENT KENNEDY ASSASSINATED

Riding in an open automobile with his wife Jacqueline, smiling and waving to huge crowds in downtown Dallas, Texas, John F. Kennedy, 46, became the fourth martyred U.S. President when struck by a sniper's rifle bullets Nov. 22, 1963.

*a* Memorial service in front of State House Nov. 25, 1963, at same time as burial in Arlington National Cemetery.

*b* Cardinal Cushing speaks with Kennedy family after saying a Memorial Mass Jan. 19, 1964. *From right:* His Eminence, Jacqueline Kennedy, Mrs. Joseph Kennedy Sr. (*Globe*/Harry Holbrook)

*b*

*c* Silver-haired Mrs. Malcolm Peabody, 72, mother of then Massachusetts Gov. Endicott Peabody, signs $450 bail bond with bondsman William Lewis April 2, 1964, after spending two nights in overcrowded St. Augustine, Fla., jail with 180 other demonstrators arrested for protesting segregation in that old slave-market municipality. (AP)

*c*

*a*

**a**   Theodore "Ted" Williams, 6 feet 4, practiced batting from childhood, joined the Red Sox in 1937, in 1941 became the last man to hit .400... In 1946 led the Red Sox to their first pennant in 28 years, at 40 won his sixth batting championship title in 1958. (*Globe*/Paul Maguire)

**b**   Olympic high jumper John Thomas, 6 feet 5, Boston University track star and later coach, jumped seven feet or higher at least 190 times, won bronze and silver Olympic medals in 1960 and 1964 and won eight national titles. He cleared a stunning 7 feet 3 indoors and 7 feet 3¾ outdoors.

**c**   Bob Cousy, 6 feet 1½, a magician in handling a basketball, was leader in his Holy Cross team's 26-game winning streak, as he was for the Boston Celtics, taking the championship in 1957 and wins, from 1959 to 1963, when he retired. (George Woodruff)

b

c

a

*a*  Bellflower Street fire, whipped by 20-mile wind gusting to 30, swept through a 3-decker tenement section of Dorchester in late afternoon, May 22, 1964 leveling 19 structures, damaging 15, injuring 256 men, women and children, leaving 300 homeless. (*Globe*/Joseph Runci)

*b*  Power failure for nearly four hours blacked out the whole Northeast, a fifth of the nation's people, Nov. 9, 1965. Planes had to land by auto headlights, stalled elevators trapped thousands, emergency operations depended on improvised lights. Only illumination at downtown Boston's Tremont and Stuart streets came from floodlights on truck, intended for a movie premiere.

*c*  Exceeding the Brink's robbery total, a machine gun-wielding gang got $1,458,000 in cash being transported in a U.S. mail truck from mid-Cape Cod banks to Boston's Federal Reserve. Late on Aug. 14, 1962 on the northbound lane of Rte. 3, Plymouth By-Pass, they hijacked the truck and its two postal employees. Crime is still unsolved. Scene: Police examining the truck. (AP)

*d*  "Boston Strangler" Albert DeSalvo, 35, who claimed to have strangled 13 women, was sentenced Jan. 18, 1967 to life imprisonment for unrelated robberies, assaults and sex offenses against four Greater Boston housewives. Nearly seven years later he was stabbed to death in Walpole Prison infirmary.

b

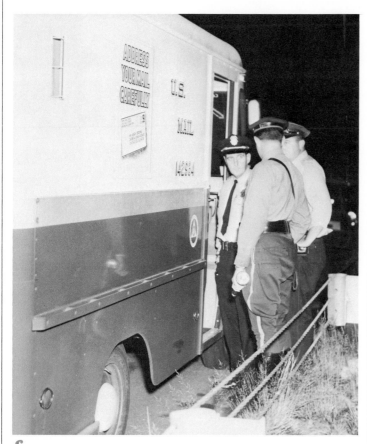

c

d

*a*

*b*

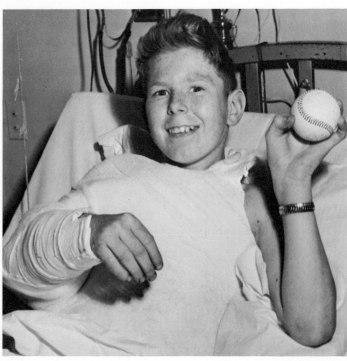

*c*

*a* Yaz – Carl Yastrzemski, Red Sox outfielder, who played baseball from childhood through Notre Dame, when 24 became the batting champion of the American league in 1963 after three years with the Red Sox. In 1967 Yaz was chosen the league's Most Valuable Player, and by 1970 had won the league's slugging championship for the third time.

*b* Defenseman Bobby Orr, who joined the Boston Bruins in 1966 when he was 18, led forays up the ice in 1969-70 that clinched their first Stanley Cup in 28 years – and in 1972 led them to their second championship, scoring the winning goal as fans thundered their applause.

*c* Six hours in operating room rejoined the right arm of redheaded 12-year-old Everett Knowles of Somerville after it was completely severed at the shoulder in a train accident May 23, 1962. The surgery was undertaken 90 minutes later at the Massachusetts General Hospital by a team headed by Dr. Ronald A. Malt. Baseball fan Everett (he later took up tennis) en route to recovery.

*d* Bill Russell, 6 feet 9, lightning fast and with fabulous control over the ball, led the Celtics to 11 N.B.A. victories, eight of them in a row. Scene: Russell leaps high for rebound as San Francisco Warriors close on him in N.B.A. game at Boston Garden Jan. 22, 1965. (AP)

*d*

*a*

*b*

c

d

a

b

*a*   Widow of Senator Robert F. Kennedy, escorted by son Robert Jr. and family, leaves St. Patrick's Cathedral after funeral service for the Senator, who was assassinated three days earlier on June 5, 1968 in a Los Angeles Hotel, where he had just thanked campaign workers on his victory that day in the California presidential primaries. (AP)

*b*   Five-hundred SDS (Students for a Democratic Society) seized University Hall, in the center of the Harvard Yard, April 9, 1969 to demand an end to Reserve Officer Training at Harvard, roughing up and ejecting Harvard deans. At 5 a.m. next day police with clubs took 20 minutes to clear them out in a bloody melee with some 45 injured and 196 arrests. Scene: Protesters fleeing through side windows. (*Globe*/Joseph Dennehy)

*c*   Three Penn Central diesels, with nobody aboard, crashed a link fence and gouged a trench three feet deep, 10 feet wide in Boston's Southeast Expressway at 3 p.m. Aug 21, 1969 just before the rush hours. No one was hurt, but the traffic tie-up was monumental and northbound lanes were closed until 4 a.m. (*Globe*/ Tom Landers)

*d*   Chappaquiddick inquest – Senator Edward M. Kennedy arrives Jan. 5, 1970 at Dukes County Courthouse for inquiry into July 19, 1969 automobile accident on Dike Bridge, Martha's Vineyard, in which he escaped death but a passenger, Miss Mary Jo Kopechne, was trapped in the submerged vehicle and drowned. (UPI)

*c*

*d*

*a*   New England's tallest building — Traditional topping-off ceremony, placement of an evergreen tree, is cooly handled 790 feet above ground level by construction worker Jimmy Conley Oct. 8, 1971 after top metal support was put in place for the 60-story John Hancock Insurance Company building in Boston's Back Bay. (Russ Adams)

*b*   Rev. Daniel Berrigan, 49, underground since April 9th to avoid prison for burning draft records in 1968, was captured Aug. 11, 1970 at his hideaway on Block Island, handcuffed and brought by FBI agents to the Federal Building, Providence, R.I. (UPI)

*c*   Younger voters, 18, 19 and 20 years old register Aug. 25, 1971 for the first time at Boston City Hall under the 26th Amendment, approved June 29, 1971. Election officials estimated 15,000 of them were eligible to vote in the mayoral election in November, 1971. (*Globe*/Bob Dean)

b

c

*a*    Boston's worst loss of firemen — Nine firemen lost their lives and eight were injured at 4-alarm fire in the roaring collapse of a corner of the 7-story former Hotel Vendome, famous Back Bay hostelry, June 17, 1972. (UPI)

*b*    Only a 20-year-old Air Force sergeant on his way from Vermont to duty in Alaska survived of 89 passengers and crew on the twin-engined Delta DC9 jetliner that struck a seawall at the foot of a fog-shrouded runway at Logan Airport July 31, 1973 in Boston's worst aviation tragedy. The sergeant died 133 days later. (*Globe*/Joseph Dennehy)

*c*    FBI's biggest arson case — $11 million fire razes Sponge Rubber Products Co.'s two-block-long plant at Shelton, Conn. March 1, 1975 following abduction of watchmen and three firebombings, leaving 900 jobless. (AP)

*a*

b

c

a

b

c

## EMINENT IN
## NEW ENGLAND

*a*    Andrew Wyeth, born 1917 at Chadds Ford, Pa., son of noted illustrator N.C. Wyeth, has brought new light and realism to his paintings of people and landscapes of Pennsylvania, New England and especially Maine. Most popular among his paintings, and exhibited in many museums, is "Christina's World."

*b*    Ruth Gordon, born 1896 in Wollaston, Mass., has been an actress, playwright, interpreter of eccentric characters on stage, in film and TV. Her Mrs. Levi in Thornton Wilder's "The Matchmaker" brought great success here and in Great Britain. "Rosemary's Baby" brought an Academy Award, and her hit roles on TV include "The American Dream."

*c*    Edwin O'Connor (1918-1968) richly presented Irish-American life in his novels. Irrepressible Frank Skeffington in *The Last Hurrah* had Mayor and Gov. James M. Curley as a fascinating model, and *Edge of Sadness,* tale of an Irish-American family, won the Pulitzer Prize in 1961.

*d*    Elma Lewis, born in Boston 1921, creator of one of the nation's largest Black cultural centers. A dynamic teacher and leader, she established the Elma Lewis School of Fine Arts Jan. 30, 1950 in a small apartment. By 1968 she had moved to the large former Temple Mishkan Tefila in Roxbury, a gift of the Combined Jewish Philanthropies, to provide community activities and teaching in music, drama and dance for hundreds of pupils.

*e*    Arthur Fiedler, born 1894 in Boston and son of a musician, moved from violin and piano to conducting. He inaugurated Boston's esplanade concerts in 1929 and the following year began to conduct the Boston Symphony's "Pop" concerts which began in 1885.

*f*    Sarah Caldwell, born 1928 in Missouri, sparked the enthusiasm that produced the Boston Opera Company and is providing it with a converted opera house. With conducting skills sharpened at the New England Conservatory of Music and the Berkshire Music Center, she organized an opera workshop at Boston University. Opera choices from Mozart to Schonberg and her insistence on quality have brought the world's top stars to her stage.

d

e

f

*a*   New England's first woman governor, U.S. Representative Ella T. Grasso, 55, Connecticut's Secretary of State for 12 years, and two-term Congressman, relaxes at her Windsor Locks, Conn., home and reads next day about her landslide victory on Nov. 5, 1974 as Connecticut's new chief executive. (AP)

*b*   "Saturday Night Massacre" — Harvard prof. Archibald Cox, special Watergate prosecutor, was fired Oct. 20, 1973 by President Nixon for insisting that Nixon make available the secret Watergate tapes, whereupon, carrying out his commitment to Congress, Cox's boss, Atty. Gen. Elliot L. Richardson, quit Nixon's cabinet. (AP)

*c*   Abortion conviction reversed — Dr. Kenneth C. Edelin, 36, convicted of manslaughter Feb. 15, 1975 in the death of a male fetus during a legal abortion on a 17-year-old woman at the Boston City Hospital, was completely cleared of all charges by the Massachusetts Supreme Judicial Court Dec. 17, 1976 in overturning the Suffolk County verdict.

*d*   Motorcycle police escort bused pupils to South Boston High School annex as a plan, ordered by the Federal Court after nine years of legal battles over school integration, took effect Sept. 12, 1974. Opening days, generally peaceful, were followed by intermittent boycotts, clashes and arrests before tensions abated. (*Globe*/Joseph Dennehy)

*e*   For the fourth time a protest on the same site was accompanied by arrests when New Hampshire State Troopers removed 176 men and women demonstrating Aug. 22, 1976 against a billion-dollar nuclear power plant at Seabrook, N.H., and charged them with trespass. Many were dragged 50 yards to waiting buses while others on the ground awaited their turn. (AP)

a

b

c